Sep 19/69

Equality

The purpose of this series is to demonstrate, through the treatment of problems drawn from contemporary life, the practical relevance of philosophy. The aim is to show how philosophical problems can arise out of, and can exert a profound influence upon, our personal and social problems; and how philosophical analysis can enlighten our moral attitudes, aspirations and decisions. At the same time, since the authors all in fact belong to the liberal, empiricist tradition of British thought, their attempts to show philosophy at work are also attempts to re-express, in a form that fits the time, the liberal vision of man and society.

PHILOSOPHY AT WORK

General Editor: Patrick Corbett

*Professor of Philosophy
at the University of Sussex*

PHILOSOPHY AT WORK

General Editor: Patrick Corbett

Ideologies
Patrick Corbett, University of Sussex

Sexual Morality
Ronald Atkinson, University of Keele

Equality
John Wilson, Farmington Trust Research Unit, Oxford

Crime and Punishment
Ted Honderich, University College, London

God and Philosophy
Antony Flew, University of Keele

War and Morality
W. B. Gallie, Queen's University, Belfast

Equality

JOHN WILSON

Director of the
Farmington Trust Research Unit, Oxford

HUTCHINSON OF LONDON

HUTCHINSON & CO (*Publishers*) LTD

178–202 Great Portland Street, London W1

London Melbourne Sydney
Auckland Bombay Toronto
Johannesburg New York

First published 1966

*This book has been set in Pilgrim, printed in Great Britain
on Antique Wove paper by Anchor Press, and
bound by Wm. Brendon, both of Tiptree, Essex*

Contents

Philosophy and Politics

A philosophical work on equality would normally be classified under the heading of 'political philosophy' or 'political theory'. The public image of this subject is in two respects inadequate. First, the image is blurred; 'political theory' is a name for nothing clear, and we are not sure what the 'political philosopher' is supposed to *do*. Secondly, the image is dull: the subject has for some time been in the doldrums, and though a breath of wind has recently been stirring its sails, it is not yet easy to see which way the wind is blowing. These two points are connected, and raise very complex problems: but I must try to say something about them here, so that the reader may gain some idea of what sort of book this is supposed to be.

One possible reason, amongst many, why political philosophy is or has been lifeless derives from the nature of some recent analytic philosophy: what most people still call 'linguistic philosophy', and what J. L. Austin suggested might be called 'linguistic phenomenology'.[1] He thereby drew attention to one important feature, perhaps the corner-stone, of the method of this kind of philosophy. An analytic philosopher is not, as the accusation still runs, 'just concerned with words'. He is concerned with words as shedding light on things (or the phenomena, or reality, or what you will). Words are not his subject-matter but his method. He works by continual cross-reference, moving from a situation in real life to the words we might use to describe it, back again to the situation, then back again to the words, and so forth. In the process both the situation and the description

1. J. L. Austin *Philosophical Papers* (O.U.P.), p. 130.

become clearer and can be better matched: and a number of puzzles, problems, and doubts can be resolved. There is a similarity here—though there are also differences—with the study of literature. By moving back and forth between the writing of a perceptive novelist and the behaviour of people in real life we learn to understand people better: we see them more clearly, and we see more in them. We also learn to value good novels. They may be stories, but they are not *just* stories. They teach us about people.

But the method of moving back and forth between language and life will only work, as a means of gaining clarity, if we start by being reasonably clear about at least *one* of these two realms. By directing our attention to ordinary, everyday situations, and the words we should naturally use in those situations, the philosopher hopes to make us feel at home, so that we can then proceed confidently and without bewitchment or confusion to other cases. Now this only works if the philosopher himself, and his audience, either have themselves experienced such situations or can readily and confidently imagine them. They have to feel at home in these situations at least: otherwise there is nowhere they can feel at home, and the whole method breaks down.

But there are plenty of situations in real life where we do not feel at home: or where some of us feel at home and others do not. Consider religious doubt, romantic love, being a dictator, feeling world-weary. It is not just that we cannot pin-point the words which could best describe these situations: it is that we cannot really pin-point the situations themselves. Perhaps it is the business of the psychologist or the novelist to help us here, or the business of philosophers of a different persuasion. To suggest this limitation for analytic philosophy is not in any sense to condemn it. One man's job is not vitiated by another's. But perhaps this helps to explain why the analytic philosophers have been widely regarded as disappointing, and why they may have been disappointing even to themselves in the realm of political philosophy.

For as that realm has usually been delimited it includes many situations with which most of us are totally unfamiliar. Political philosophy has been traditionally concerned with concepts like natural law, sovereignty, the social contract, the state, the general will, and so forth. These concepts relate, putting it roughly, to the experience of politicians or administrators rather than of ordinary people. They relate to the process of government in a sovereign state: and most of us are not concerned with government. We may indeed, particularly if we live in a country which has not (as England has) a fairly long tradition of secure and stable rule, be concerned with government in the sense that we are concerned very passionately with who governs us. But we do not find ourselves in governmental positions. By contrast, we cannot avoid finding ourselves in moral positions: and the philosopher can use these, as part of his method, to help us do moral philosophy. But politics, like aesthetics, is not in this sense a necessary activity for all men.

But if the realm of political philosophy were redefined, so that the concepts can be related to common rather than minority experience, the basis for this criticism would be removed. Few of us are ever aware of being in conflict with 'the state', or indeed ever had occasion to think about it very much. But nearly all of us have some experience of 'the boss', 'the family', or 'the authorities'. Perhaps philosophy suffers because we have wrongly delimited the area of politics itself.

By saying 'wrongly delimited' I do not imply that there is a 'real' realm of politics, ideally and absolutely fixed, to which alone the label of 'politics' can be properly tied. But it seems possible that our notion of political theory has never really recovered from its treatment at the hands of Plato and Aristotle. Living in small and virtually self-contained city-states, the Greeks of the classical period would have hotly and rightly denied that they did not come into conflict with 'the state' or that they rarely even thought about it. The city-state was small and manageable enough, and its free citizens had enough leisure and enough room for political manœuvre, for 'the state' to be as real to them as 'the boss' or 'the neighbours' are to us. Today we live not only within much larger, more powerful, and more complex sovereign states but also under the shadow of even more giant-like and incomprehensible power blocks. Yet there has been a tacit assumption that political theories can still be profitably discussed in the same terms of reference.

As one might expect, ordinary language has reflected the change in our situation. 'Politics' in English is only a shadow of what Aristotle meant by '*politike*'. The remaining substance is filled up today with a number of cognate disciplines: law and economics are obvious examples. A more important example from our point of view is the comparatively new discipline of sociology. We can see ourselves in sociological territory if we reflect that many of the questions traditionally asked about 'the state' might today be more realistically asked about smaller communities which are more real to us —'the school', 'the regiment', 'the firm', 'the village', or 'the family'. The sovereign state is in some logical respects a unique society, but it is not the only society which can generate philosophical problems: nor is it clear that it is always the most important society in our everyday lives. If we adopt a much wider sense of 'politics', whereby politics is concerned with the organisation and power of a number of individuals or groups in relation to each other, then it is immediately plain that we face political situations every day, both in our private and our public lives.

Without going more deeply into this problem I hope at least to have shown that concepts like equality can be relevant to situations other than those which have been the stock-in-trade of traditional political philosophy: and I shall endeavour to use some of those situations to elucidate the concept of equality. But, since I shall be using, for the most part, the methods of modern analytic philosophy, it may also be necessary to issue a warning. If philosophy is any good at all it cannot be any good as a kind of amateur sociology, or as a way of advocating some particular political or moral creed. That is not its job. Its job is to put the reader in a better position to judge these things for himself. It does this job primarily by clarification: by showing the work that the concept of equality has done, and does, and could do. A lot of what follows, therefore, may seem much drier than this introduction would suggest. If it is too dry, it will be my fault. But it is worth remembering that, to many people, mathematics is drier than flying aeroplanes: and that if there had been no mathematics there would be no aeroplanes to fly.

It may help the reader if I say why I think that this kind of philosophy has both a general importance and also a particular importance to our society at this time. To describe political philosophy as the 'clarification of concepts' may still suggest that its purpose and effect are largely academic rather than practical. But this can only be because we think either that we need not use concepts like equality at all in practical living or that we can use them perfectly well by ourselves without having them clarified by philosophers. Neither of these views is plausible. In so far as politics is not mere power-seeking and chicanery, politicians have to make use of abstract concepts, such as justice, democracy, liberty, and so forth: and the principles behind the concepts are ones which we all use in family life, at the office, in friendship, love affairs, committees, and so on. We cannot *help* thinking in some such terms. Similarly, one has only to consider the immense differences in the way different people deploy the concepts to see that they stand in need of clarification. In Communist countries they talk of 'democracy' just as we do: but they plainly mean something different. In our own society different political groups demand 'justice' and 'equality of opportunity': but it is not clear just *what* they are demanding when they use these terms.

Clarification has both a negative and a positive role. Its negative role is to prevent confusion: to stop people using words just anyhow: to enable us to understand each other and hence to communicate properly. Its positive role consists in the fact that out of this analysis certain ideas which have been veiled by the general confusion become clear: and these ideas may have considerable practical value. Thus I hope to show, by a careful analysis of what people have meant by 'equality' and of the way in which it interlocks with other concepts such as justice and liberty, that there is at least one sort of equality which has been, as it were, latent in our thinking and which has great importance not only for politics in the narrow sense but for all personal relationships. But I do not wish simply to grab hold of this idea, label it 'equality', and try to sell it to everybody in the same way that a propagandist might try to sell it. For, as I have said, the idea is *latent* in everyone's mind: it is, in a sense, something which we all know already, but of which we need to be made fully conscious. And this can only be done by considering our thinking about equality carefully and in detail.

The philosopher's business in this respect is not unlike the psychoanalyst's. The psychoanalyst's job is not to tell the patient what to think, to sell him one particular moral idea or way of life. He has to help the patient to work through the patient's thinking and feeling in detail, so that eventually the patient can come to see things clearly for himself. The logical analyst's job is different only in that he works on the language we use, rather than directly on the emotions and behaviour we display. The two disciplines are nevertheless closely interlinked. In each case the aim is to make the person more self-conscious, more able to see his thought from the outside, and hence more capable of freeing himself from bewitchment. For both our language and our behaviour can be bewitched—dominated by certain kinds of compulsion which prevent us from seeing clearly. The philosopher, like the psychoanalyst, should be a liberator rather than a moralist.[1]

If we engage in politics, whether in the narrow or the wide sense of the word, we cannot help but adopt some attitude towards other people, and this attitude cannot help but find expression in some language, however primitive. This is the general reason why political philosophy is important. In just the same way, if we are going to build a pyramid or a bridge, we are bound to use some kind of mathematics, even if it is only a rough-and-ready rule-of-thumb calculation. To call mathematics 'academic' or 'impractical' is today plainly absurd. But it might have *seemed* less absurd, though it would not really have been so, before the importance of mathematics for science and engineering was appreciated. As soon as people seriously wished to do things like science and engineering they found that mathematics was essential.

This suggests a particular reason why political philosophy is important today. Politics in the narrow sense, and relationships within human groups also, have until recently not been regarded as a suitable subject for any kind of scientific approach. Politics has been largely a struggle for power and the history of conflicting pressure-groups: and personal relationships have been conducted by rule of thumb, guess-

1. See also pp. 147–52

work, doctrinaire ideals, and various kinds of emotional impulse. Recently, however, we have in our society achieved sufficient mastery over nature to allow us somewhat more leisure for rational consideration. There is still plenty to fight about, but phenomena such as gross tyranny, forcible oppression, starvation, and civil war are for certain societies—so at least we hope—things of the past. One of the reasons why there seems to be little idealism in politics today, even on the left wing, is perhaps that the reforming politicians have worn out their weapons in achieving victory, and have not yet forged new ones. In a time of affluence we need different kinds of ideals, ideals of a sociological rather than an economic kind.

Freed to some extent from a politics of brute force and conflicting interests, and encouraged by the rise of sociology and psychology, we may be entering upon an age in which relationships within sovereign states and within other groups can be studied objectively, *and in which this sort of study will have practical effect.* Under such circumstances political philosophy is peculiarly important. Different political philosophies were often in the past little more than the strong feelings of certain groups of people who wanted certain specific things, and who dressed up their feelings in philosophical guise in order to make them look impressive. In such violent situations the political philosopher who clarified rather than propagandised may well have been a voice crying in the wilderness. But if we are adopting a more objective and scientific approach to society we may genuinely want the philosopher to clarify, rather than provide us with some high-sounding words in which to dress up a practical programme on which we have already decided.

At this time, not only in England but in all technologically advanced societies, there is a great need of new ideals and a new sense of purpose. Such ideals and such a sense cannot be invented out of the blue, so to speak: nor, if we are wise, will we allow them simply to develop, haphazardly and without our conscious control, out of some particular situation that overtakes us. That would be to go back to the time of violence, in which changes in society were not our own work but virtually forced on us by economic and other social conditions. We want to be our own masters. We are compelled, therefore, to take the language in which we think with the utmost seriousness: and, by constant cross-reference between our talk and practical social situations, to see if we can elicit from our own minds some ideal which will be a guide for the future.[1]

1. Further remarks on this topic will be found in the Epilogue.

Introduction

1 Some Possible Roles for the Concept of Equality

There is an old joke about a man who went to a psychiatrist to be cured of an inferiority complex. After studying his case the psychiatrist dismissed him with the words 'I'm sorry, Mr. Jones, but you just *are* inferior'.

This is not a very funny joke, but it is fairly funny. The fact that it is funny bears witness to a kind of tension or ambivalence of feeling which most of us have towards human beings. On the one hand, we feel inclined to assert some basic human equality: we say things like 'All men are equal' or 'One man's as good as another'. We might say also that, whatever their different skills and talents and merits, all human beings were of equal worth, or equally valuable, or equal in the eyes of God. But if this were all we thought, the joke would not be funny, because the psychiatrist would just be making a stupid mistake. On the other hand, we sometimes feel that there are some people who 'just *are* inferior': people who are hopelessly incompetent, stupid, lazy, unlovable, and shiftless. We sometimes say, not just that such people are 'no good at anything' but even that they are 'no good' in general. But if this were all we thought, the joke would not be funny either, because the psychiatrist —assuming that he knew his job—would be obviously right.

Both these feelings are important. It is fatally easy to try to deny one or the other of them: but this abolishes the problem rather than solves it. We ourselves live in an age and a society in which the first of these two feelings is considered the more respectable. We are our 'better selves' when we assert the equality of all men: and when we catch ourselves

giving vent to the other feeling we are apt to regard it as
prejudice or cynicism. Most of us are against colour- and
class-prejudice, we dislike anti-Semitism, we are in favour
of treating women as equals, we believe in helping under-
developed countries. Yet in hard-headed moods we say things
like 'Ah, but if you'd lived amongst the natives as I have,
you'd think differently' or 'But the fact is that women *like*
to be told what to do by men'. Most arguments about
equality are not much more than the expression of these two
moods.

I have begun by putting the problem in terms of a conflict
of feeling because misrepresentation tends to happen at a
very early stage, before the business of philosophical analysis has got properly started. Any honest analysis must begin
by trying to understand what people mean when they say
things: but an analyst will tend to interpret what people
say in the light of the sort of things he says himself. Thus, if
you are hard-headed rather than high-minded, you probably
do not go around saying things like 'All men are equal' or
'We are all equal in God's sight' or 'No man is of more value
than any other'. You will be apt to interpret these remarks,
which look like statements of fact, in some other way which
appears to you more respectable. On the other hand, if you
are of a metaphysical turn of mind, you will resist any
attempt to claim that such statements are not what they
seem. You might believe them to be statements of fact, just
as 'All men are bipeds' is a statement of fact. In order, therefore, to avoid prejudging the question of what logical status
we can assign to the things people say about equality, it is
worth suggesting certain categories into which what they say
might fall.

One good way of trying to avoid prejudice is simply to
notice various things about the meaning of the word 'equal'
and of other words that seem closely connected with it,
without trying to fit them into any preconceived theory. The
Oxford English Dictionary gives the following meanings,
amongst others, under 'equal': '1. Identical in amount, magnitude, number, value, intensity, etc.: neither less nor
greater. 2. Possessing a like degree of a quality or attribute;
on the same level in dignity, power, excellence, etc.; having

the same rights or privileges.' The meaning 'fair, equitable, impartial' is given as obsolete: but under 'equity' is given 'the quality of being equal'—a rather curious definition—'or fair; impartiality; even-handed dealing'.

From this it is plain that the concept of equality is by no means a simple one. We have before us, it seems, a number of interlocking ideas, closely related to each other, yet perhaps distinguishable: and it is not clear just which ideas are normally or most usefully expressed by the word 'equality'. A study of other languages reveals the same closely knit framework of thought and language. Thus the Latin '*aequus*', from which are derived the words for 'equal' in the Romance languages as well as in our own, can be used to mean 'level' or 'flat', 'balanced', 'fair' or 'just', 'uniform' (like our own 'equable'), or just 'similar' (like the German '*gleich*'). Which of these meanings is, philologically speaking, the root or basic meaning is uncertain. What is important is that, in most if not all human societies, these different meanings have seemed so akin to each other that they are often borne by the same word.

One curiosity about the word 'equal' is that we can usually distinguish between those words which in our society carry an element of value with them and are normally used as words of praise, and those words which are purely descriptive and not commendatory. Amongst the first are 'fair', 'just', 'equitable'; among the second are 'similar', 'identical', 'uniform', and 'level'. Not a few words are on the borderline, and their significance depends very much on the speaker and the context. Thus 'equable' and 'consistent' are often used as terms of praise when we are talking of a man's character or behaviour, as is also the word 'balance': and 'impartial' is nearly always a value-word. 'Equal' *may* sometimes be used, even nowadays, as a word of praise: but in general it is purely descriptive. It would be natural to demand justice or equity *as of right*: these are things which by definition people ought to have. But whereas 'Justice, O King!' is natural, 'Equality, O King!' is not.

Now this is curious, because many—perhaps most—political and moral concepts of long standing have managed to acquire some kind of halo: they carry with them the implication that the state of affairs they describe is, at least *prima facie*, desirable. 'Justice', 'fairness', 'liberty', and 'fraternity' in politics, like 'honour', 'integrity', 'honesty', and 'loyalty' in morality, are all terms of praise. But the case is different with equality. Some people believe in it (whatever it is), others do not: there may be fashions for or against it, but no fashion seems to have lasted long enough to leave its mark on our language by putting a halo on the word.

The reason for this might simply be, as I have implied, that there does not happen to have been a sufficiently long-established social tradition of equality to give it a halo. But it may also be that the notion of equality *lies further back*, so to speak, in our political and moral thinking, than other notions which have been more easily grasped and hence more readily sanctified. We are apt to regard equality in the light of the history of liberalism, as one star in a constellation of concepts, shining alongside of fraternity, liberty, and democracy. But this picture may misrepresent the position, and it does not account for the fact that 'equality' is primarily, at least, a descriptive and not an evaluative term. It may be more reasonable to suppose that equality is the corner-stone of a building whose more obvious features are made up of other political concepts: that the notion of equality, just because it is descriptive, is the essential point of departure of the road to liberalism. The chapters that follow should go some way towards substantiating this point.

The fact that 'equal' is a descriptive term, and yet has close connections with evaluative terms such as 'fair', 'just' or 'impartial', poses us another problem. Some sentences in which reference is made to equality are plainly intended as recommendations, or slogans, or assertions of moral principle —as when we say 'People *ought to be* treated equally' or 'Equal pay for equal work!' (sc. 'is a *good* thing') or 'It is *right* to love all your children equally'. There may still be difficulties about how to interpret parts of these sentences, but at least we know that their general intention is to recommend and not to state facts. Other sentences, however, such as 'All men are equal', *look* like statements of fact. But are they? For (we might argue) what empirical facts can 'All men are equal' conceivably assert? Certainly it does not specifically assert any: it does not say that men are equal in any specific respect. And if we consider any specific respect it might appear that men are not equal. They are not precisely similar in respect of their size, intelligence, needs, will-power, saintliness, or any other natural quality: and there have been, and could always be, societies in which their rights, powers, social roles, and status were also totally dissimilar. Hence we might feel inclined to *translate* 'All men are equal' into some other form: perhaps into 'all men should be treated equally', which is prescriptive rather than factual. This temptation is strengthened by the very close connections between the descriptive senses of 'equal' and its evaluative senses. Thus we might suppose that when people talk about equality in a political or moral context what they really mean to talk about is some closely related evaluative concept, such as impartiality or justice.

These and other translations are interesting and important; but as *full translations* they will not work because they do not represent the intentions of the speaker in the way that the original 'all men are equal' represented them. The characteristic argument of those who assert human equality is roughly of the form: 'All men are equal: and *therefore* they ought to be treated equally' (or 'therefore the colour bar is bad', or 'therefore you have to give very good reasons for different treatment'). This is supposed to be an *argument*: 'therefore' is supposed to mean something. To use a parallel, Christians argue that we ought to love each other because God is love, and we are his children. Now it might well be thought that Christians have invented the premises of this argument: that they have invented a God whose children we are. And it may also be true that the psychological motivation for this invention was the desire, conscious or unconscious, to end up with the belief that we ought to love each other. But this has to be proved: and it will not do to suggest that all Christians are 'really saying' when they make factual assertions about God is that we ought to love each other. Similarly it may be that there is no such thing as basic human equality, in the sense (whatever this is) that 'All men are equal' is intended to bear. But it is certainly intended to bear this sense. It might be possible to show the assertion to be meaningless or mistaken: but it is hardly possible to show it to be a mere masquerade. The philosopher's job is to give such assertions a clear sense *which is also the sense they are intended to bear.* And one good test for this is whether the feelings of those who advance such metaphysics are satisfied. This has to be done not merely by showing them that there are certain things that they cannot rationally or sensibly assert, but also by showing them new and better ways of expressing those feelings. We have to clarify the metaphysics of equality *without loss.*

I intend this merely as an illustration of the dangers of over-hasty translation, or of supposing that any one translation is likely to be sufficient. It does not at all follow that attempts at translation are a waste of time: for we might reasonably hope that by offering enough different translations we could do full justice to the intentions of those who made the original assertions about equality. (Thus, it may indeed be that on some occasions 'All men are equal' *is* intended to mean no more than 'all men should be treated equally'.) It is perfectly reasonable to put the original assertions into different clothes, as it were, and see where they are most comfortable: all we have to guard against is putting them into a straitjacket.

2 *Summary of the Argument*

In what follows I have had to take the bull by the horns and divide the possible roles played by assertions about equality into four general categories, to each of which I devote one part of the book. To begin with (1) we shall consider equality as a *political principle*. This will help us both to get the feel of the concept, by looking at practical cases, and also to elucidate the logic of the principle, by pressing these cases to their limits and observing the assumptions that lie behind them. Next (2) we shall try to make sense of assertions like 'All men are equal' as *assertions of fact* rather than as moral or political judgements of value. Then (3) we shall consider equality as representing what I shall call a *formal principle*: that is, a logical characteristic or a logical rule which defines certain kinds of thought or discourse. Here we shall be particularly concerned with the notion of impartiality as a necessary condition of moral or political theory. Finally (4) we shall look at equality as representing an *ideal*—some state of affairs considered to be desirable, rather than a rule or

principle or fact: and I shall try to show that it is this role
which is central, and gives importance to the other three
roles. We shall conclude (5) with some examples in which I
shall try to apply what we have learnt to practical cases in
society and in our personal relationships,

Since the first four parts are intended as a coherent thesis,
in which the argument is cumulative and not just a series of
independent and isolated points, it may help the reader if I
give here a brief account of why I have chosen to concentrate on these particular roles for the notion of equality,
and arrayed them in the order described just above: that is,
(1) equality as a political principle, (2) equality as a fact, (3)
equality as a formal principle, and (4) equality as an ideal.

The general question I am trying to answer may crudely
be phrased thus: 'What is it that believers in equality, and
liberals in general, really have to sell?' To this question most
of the best modern philosophers have given two types of
answer. First, they have shown how demands for equality,
in the history of politics and human society, vary in their
significance from one context to another. What the egalitarian has to sell depends on the particular context: it may
be that he wants to abolish race prejudice and introduce
racial equality, or to abolish a capitalist system and introduce
equality of incomes, or to abolish a patriarchal society and
introduce equality of the sexes. But there may be no *general*
political principle of equality which the egalitarian is trying
to sell: and there may be no factual sense in which all men
are equal, on which the egalitarian can rely in any context.
Secondly, philosophers have shown how the egalitarian may
be pointing, not to any metaphysical truth about the equality
of all men, nor yet to any important moral ideal which can
be rationally defended, but to certain important logical
features which are characteristic of certain kinds of discourse: namely, to the notions of impartiality and consistency in following moral rules. In other words, the egalitarian is drawing attention to a purely logical or *formal*
principle, not to any kind of metaphysical truth or ideal.

Both these approaches are important: but I believe that
the egalitarian has more to sell than these philosophers
allow. Underlying both the particular political demands, and
the formal principles of impartiality and consistency which

characterise moral discourse, there is an ideal and a metaphysical truth which can be rationally defended by reference to human nature, and which alone give point and purpose to political demands and formal principles. It is this truth and this ideal that egalitarians and liberals really want to sell. I should be the first to agree that they have not given a very clear account of why we should buy, and it is perhaps partly for this reason that some contemporary philosophers (as I think) have been too hasty in dismissing their sales talk.

Thus in our consideration of equality as a political principle in Part One, it will become clear that there is more to demands for equality than is given by the particular requirements of particular political situations. Behind these specific demands, in other words, lies some kind of metaphysical view about the 'natural' equality of all human beings. A good many views about 'natural' equality will not hold water; and these I criticise in Part One. In Part Two I endeavour to get at the root of this metaphysical belief, and to say just what it is about human beings which would justify granting them some kind of 'natural' equality. This has to do with the fact that they have wills of their own, and can choose and create their own values. This fact alone, however, although it may give sense to the notion of human equality, cannot sufficiently justify the kind of liberalism that egalitarians have traditionally supported: further argument is needed. Hence in Part Three I turn to the more formal topic of moral language, to see whether the notion of equality is presupposed by moral discourse itself. We perceive that this is not so: despite the importance of moral language, which shows that the idea of following rules impartially is a necessary logical feature of morality itself, any substantial moral rules or principles must be derived from some moral *ideal*. Although the ideals of equality, liberty, democracy, and other liberal notions may seem to us more obviously sensible than authoritarian or totalitarian ideals, we have still not done enough to show that they must commend themselves to all rational people. In Part Four I try to solve this problem, and to lay the basis for liberal theory in general and equality in particular. Beginning with the notions of rationality and choice, I suggest that criteria similar to those which we use for judging sanity (or rationality in a wide sense of the word) may also be used to justify a liberal outlook. The chief of these criteria is to be found in the notion of communication or fraternity: the ability to identify with other people, to communicate with them in a fraternal way, as equals, rather than to have a master-slave relationship with them, is what lies at the root of liberalism. This argument enables us to capitalise on the 'natural' equality outlined in Part Two: it can now be seen that this 'natural' equality must, for all rational creatures, be a paramount consideration in their moral outlook. The egalitarian arguments of Part One, and the formal considerations of Part Three, should now fall into place behind this central notion of communication.

This means, to put it rather crudely, that the reader will have to wait for the really basic arguments until Part Four. But my purpose is to show, in the first three parts, how the traditional views about equality, liberalism, rationality, moral language, and so on seem plainly to call for some such substantial basis as I offer in Part Four. These traditional views are important in themselves, and there are a great number of crucial points that have to be made, and explanations given, as we proceed: but my chief defence of this method is that these views have to be *worked through*, as it were, before their inadequacy can be made plain, and before we can see just what sort of foundations need to be laid in order to support them.

I can only ask the reader not to grow too impatient as he proceeds. What I feel much more uncertain about is whether the foundations I produce in Part Four are in fact adequate to support the building. I think that they come from the right quarry, so to speak, but I am very doubtful whether I have shaped them with sufficient skill and strength to do the job properly. But this the reader must judge for himself.

PART ONE

EQUALITY
AS A POLITICAL
PRINCIPLE

I

Equality in Historical Contexts

a) Equality of Treatment and Equality of Scope

We must begin with a rough but important distinction. Perhaps because we are bewitched by political contexts in which underprivileged classes demand that their needs be satisfied we too often assume equality to be concerned solely with rules about what people *get* or *receive*, rather than with rules about what they can *do*. But rules and rights can be of both kinds. In the game of Monopoly each player has the right to receive a 'salary' on passing 'Go', but also has the right to do certain things of his own choosing, such as building a house on his property or not doing so, staying in jail for three turns or paying a fine to come out at once, and so on. Not only are all the players treated equally: they have equal scope. It is not only a matter of their being equally catered for, but also a matter of their being allowed to deploy their wills and their intiative equally in certain ways.

Thus, if we said to a doctor in charge of a hospital ward, 'Treat all your patients equally', this recommendation would have something to do with what the patients *got* from the doctor. It is not clear, without further specification, exactly what they would get: it might be an equal amount of the doctor's time, or an equal degree of comfort in the ward, or an equal amount of money spent on drugs for them, or all sorts of things. But there is no question of the patients having equal scope. On the other hand, if I believe in the equality of women, and tell my married friend that he should treat his wife as an equal, the case is very different: and it is just this vagueness in the word 'treat' which may make us lose sight of the difference. I should not *only* mean by my injunction that he ought to cater for her needs with as much diligence as for his own: this might not even be my chief point. I should mean rather that her will should count for as much as his: that she should be given an equal status, not as a receiver but as an agent. Thus I should expect him above all to give her an equal voice in making decisions: to give her equal powers with himself, or equal scope. This could certainly be described as *treating* her as an equal: but the difference between this case and the doctor's emerges if we stress the phrase 'as an equal'. The doctor treats his patients equally but not as equals.

This is because the doctor is in a position of superiority by virtue of his skill, whereas the husband (according to the advice I give my friend) is not. We make a distinction between the context of medical attention, where there are experts who distribute various forms of treatment, and the context of marriage, where there is no question of expertise but simply two human beings confronting each other. In contexts of expertise people do not in the fullest sense *do* things at all: they are told what to do by the experts, or they have things done to them. Equality of scope does not arise. But if there is no expertise it is no longer simply a matter of how we treat people, but of what powers we allow them.

This last phrase is a little misleading, however, because we might be taken to imply that there is always somebody (like the husband in our example) who distributes powers and allots scope, and somebody (the wife) who simply receives and enjoys these powers. This would assimilate equality of scope much more closely to equality of treatment. There are indeed many cases where this happens. Some rulers, by virtue of a political or social tradition, are in a position of such power that they can distribute powers to other people, very much as a parent might distribute powers to his children. He may give them all equal powers, or dissimilar powers that vary according to their age or reliability or good sense. But there are other cases where we do not start off with a pre-existing tradition: or in which, though there may be a tradition, we question it in our minds so radically that the situation amounts to a fresh start. Thus, suppose some of us are wrecked on a desert island, then nobody is likely to be by tradition in a position of power, such that he can distribute powers to the rest of us: or suppose that we start a political revolution which is designed to destroy the whole traditional power-structure of our society, we might then say that all members of the society would have equal powers or equal scope without these powers being granted them by any existing authority.

Since it is hard to conceive of cases where there is absolutely no authority, we might well phrase our demand by saying that each member of a society should be *given* or *granted* equal powers, or even by saying that 'the state' should do this. But if we were genuinely making a fresh start it would be more precise to say that we should all *agree to have* the same powers. The difference is crucial. If we are inclined to accept some theory about the basic equality of human beings, e.g. as creators of their own values,[1] then we shall recognise this equality and hence negotiate with our fellows, rather than assume that we have the sole right to distribute power and hence grant it to those whom we think fit. There is a big difference between a husband who, whether graciously or ungraciously, allows his wife an equal voice in making decisions, and a husband who recognises her equality with himself as a decision-maker; and, in general, there is a sense in which human beings *have* rights, as opposed to merely being given them.

This distinction enables us to make some sense of the innumerable demands for equality that have been made in the history of politics. With many notable exceptions, of which classical Athens is the most notorious, it is fair to say that it is not until after the Renaissance that the notion of equal scope becomes really popular. Even in Athens at its most democratic it was never more than the powers of adult male citizens which were intended to be equal: slaves, women, and resident aliens did not count as people for voting purposes. Of course, this raises problems about who can properly be accounted as a person for political purposes. In England there are differences of opinion about the right to vote of those under twenty-one, criminals, new immigrants, and the mentally subnormal: and elsewhere there are problems about the voting rights of Negroes and other groups. But it is

1. As advanced in Part Two.

generally true that the last four or five centuries have witnessed a progressive widening of the franchise, which has been accompanied (or even caused) by the recognition of human beings not only as objects of treatment but as agents.

Before that time we may reasonably liken most societies to the stage of childhood in which social and moral rules concerning power or scope are accepted by the child as customary, and no question of justification arises. On the other hand, it is likely that in all societies, however primitive, the demand for at least some forms of equal treatment is always present. One reason for this may be simply that it is possible to exist as a human being without any political power or scope, but not without some minimal satisfaction of basic needs, such as the need for food and shelter, or without certain basic forms of protection, such as protection against being killed. We might say that people are interested in social rules primarily in order to avoid things like starvation or untimely death, and only secondarily in order to acquire power or scope. It may be even true that this secondary interest is based on the primary one: it is useful to have power, because this is a good way of ensuring that one's needs are satisfied. But this is not to say that other reasons cannot be advanced for giving people equal scope, reasons not necessarily connected with the satisfaction of their needs.

One obvious illustration of the point made above is the prime importance which societies attach to their first legal code: examples of this are the Code of Dracon in ancient Athens, the Twelve Tables in Rome, and Magna Carta in England. These codes were forced upon the existing authorities (oligarchs or monarchs) by social groups whose prime concern was to ensure that the authorities could not do certain things to them. Though they limit the power of the authorities, they do not necessarily give more power to the underprivileged: what they do is to lay down certain rules of treatment. This 'equality before the law', though it may not be the same equality for all social classes, represents the first step in equality of treatment. However severe or biassed the code, at least it is known *what the rules are*: at least the authorities are not allowed to treat the underprivileged just as they choose. Their power is no longer arbitrary.

Such concessions by the authorities, however, in some sense increase the power of the underprivileged inasmuch as they weaken the powers of the authorities. The underprivileged person no longer has to obey the authorities in all respects: his life is to some extent governed by impartial rules which the authorities have to abide by. Moreover, he has to some degree demonstrated or realised his power, in another sense of the word, if not increased it, precisely by extorting these concessions: and historically it is usual for such extortions to be followed not only by more concessions about treatment but also by concessions of positive power and scope. Yet the distinction, blurred though it may be in practice, still remains. It is true that the underprivileged person has shown his teeth in extorting these concessions: but what he has gained by showing his teeth, in cases like the early legal codes, is not the right to *do* anything but the right to *avoid suffering* certain things, like wanton imprisonment or murder. By showing his teeth he has made a display of natural power or force, not used a power or a degree of scope which has been allotted him.

b) *Equality and the Establishment*

Both the demand for equal treatment and the demand for equal scope, however, often threaten the established or traditional order. It is here that we can locate the struggle, common to the history of many societies, between two apparently opposing principles: the principle of equality on the one hand, and the principle of order on the other. With equality go concepts like liberty, democracy, fraternity, and the view that society should be run by mutual agreement: with the principle of order go the notions of efficiency, hierarchy, and what the Greeks called '*eunomia*' ('law and order'), as also the view that good government depends on leaving matters to those best qualified to deal with them, and on every person taking his proper station in society. The classical illustration of the former principle is in the 'state of nature' as envisaged by egalitarian philosophers such as Locke and Rousseau: of the latter, Plato's *Republic*.

Yet it is not clear that these principles are, so to speak, theoretically as well as practically opposed. In practice it may be true, as Aristotle says, that 'the weaker are always anxious for equality and justice: the strong pay no heed to either', though even this is an over-simplification. For both parties represent their case in terms of justice. In a famous speech in Shakespeare's *Troilus and Cressida* Ulysses argues for the importance of obedience to the established ruler:

> The heavens themselves, the planets, and this centre
> Observe degree, priority and place,
> Insisture, course, proportion, season, form,
> Office, and custom, in all line of order:
> And therefore is the glorious planet Sol
> In noble eminence enthroned and sphered ...
>
> Take but degree away, untune that string,
> And hark what discord follows; each thing meets
> In mere oppugnancy: the bounded waters
> Should lift their bosoms higher than the shores,
> And make a sop of all this solid globe:
> Strength should be lord of imbecility,
> And the rude son should strike his father dead:
> Force should be right; or rather, right and wrong—
> Between whose endless jar justice resides—
> Should lose their names, and so should justice too.[1]

Ulysses is arguing for 'law and order' and for obedience to the establishment: but he represents this as a principle of justice.

Compare this with the speech of Jocasta in Euripides' *Phoenissae*, in which she tries to persuade her son to share the kingship with his brother: 'Why are you so keen on status-seeking, son? Don't be, it's quite wrong—the worst possible guide for life you could have. When that idea is current in a family or a state it always ruins those who believe in it. Yet you're crazy about it! Much better to put your money on equality, my boy: that's what makes for solidarity among friends and townships and nations. Equality is what's naturally right for men, you see: when you get the overprivileged and the underprivileged lined up against each other there's always trouble. After all, the idea

1. Act I, Scene 3, lines 85–118.

of equality is responsible for things like weights and measures and mathematics; the dark night and the bright sun take an equal share all the year round—neither's jealous because it has to give way to the other. If the sun and the night are prepared to do this for men's benefit, aren't you prepared to go fifty-fifty in your inheritance with your brother? And if you don't, what happens to the idea of justice?'[1] Jocasta too is arguing for 'law and order' and for justice: but her argument, unlike Ulysses', works in favour of equality and against hierarchy.

Nature is the most obvious candidate to sponsor political ideals, whether egalitarian or anti-egalitarian. Thus Aristotle is at some pains to show that slaves, women, and children are in their different ways naturally inferior, or natural subordinates, because they lack to some degree the 'faculty of deliberation': and two thousand years later Burke writes: 'We fear God; we look up with awe to Kings; with affection to parliaments; with duty to magistrates; with reverence to priests; and with respect to nobility. Why? Because when such ideas are brought before our minds, it is *natural* to be so affected', and says that 'our political system is placed in a just correspondence and symmetry with the order of the world'. At the same time Godwin could write: 'The state of society is uncontestably artificial; the power of one man over another must be always derived from convention, or from conquest; by nature we are equal', and Locke that the law of Nature 'teaches all mankind who will but consult it, that being all equal and independent, no one ought to harm another . . .'.

The supernatural may also be used to justify such ideals: indeed, it is often hard to tell, in considering such justifications, where the natural ends and the supernatural begins. A fairly clear case, however, can be seen in the history of the Christian Church. In its early days the emphasis is on equality: the brethren of the Church were regarded as equal, and are even alleged to have had 'all things in common'. This egalitarian and proto-communist existence depended on the view that differences between men were unimportant in comparison with their equality as sons of God and brothers to each other. With the organisation of an ecclesiastical

1. Lines 531–48.

B

hierarchy, however, the emphasis rapidly changes, and writers as early as St. Paul stress the importance of obedience to the authorities. All men may still be brothers, but this limpid view becomes muddied by the introduction of men who are Fathers and women who are Mothers Superior. Splinter groups that break away from the hierarchy later in history, such as the Protestants, the Puritans, and the Nonconformists in general, attempt to revive the original egalitarianism by denying that the authorities are supernaturally sponsored. If all that counts is a man's conscience and his direct individual relationship with God, then men are equal in a stronger sense than if certain men (like the Pope) have a special pipeline to God's will. Yet even this egalitarianism may be only partial: it is not surprising to find writers like Milton, who took part in what was in some sense a revolutionary movement, maintaining the divinely appointed inequality of men and women, and describing the respective roles of Eve and Adam in the line

He for God only, she for God in him.

This may tempt us to suppose that the notions of nature or the supernatural are wholly neutral as regards equality or inequality; that they can be used indifferently for supporting either. But we gain this impression because both sides commonly refer not simply to certain brute facts in nature but to some kind of natural order: thus both Ulysses and Jocasta in our examples use the order of nature to justify different ideals. Which ideals you justify depends on which parts of the natural order you choose to stress. Ulysses stresses the dominating position of the sun over the other planets to advocate a hierarchy: Jocasta stresses the alternation of day and night to advocate equality.

The position is different if we draw attention to brute facts about human beings. It is, of course, possible, in this case also, to select facts that tell either way. We can stress the variations in height, weight, intelligence, manual skill, beauty, and so on amongst human beings, in order to justify inequality: or we can stress their similarities to justify equality. But the natural variations amongst men have generally seemed much less than the variations in the natural order as a whole: and for this reason justifications of inequality on this basis seem less convincing. By most criteria of similarity, men seem very much alike: and egalitarianism has gained ground over the centuries not so much because egalitarians have browbeaten people into accepting new criteria (when they could quite reasonably have been content with criteria which justified inequality) but rather because they have succeeded in *waking people up* to the general similarities of all men which could be recognised, with a slight mental effort, by existing criteria of similarity.

What delayed this recognition was, in part, the inability to distinguish clearly between natural and artificial equality and inequality.[1] Thus it is plain to us that kings and bishops are naturally much the same as ordinary people; their superiority is one of status, a superiority afforded them by man-made rules. But not so long ago this would not have been plain: it would have been believed that kings and bishops were somehow intrinsically different, and the support for this view would have been found in the supernatural powers or rights which they had and other men did not have. It would have been felt that 'not all the water in the rough, rude sea can wash the balm from an anointed king':[2] and in general, as St. Paul says, that 'the powers that be are ordained of God'.

This kind of metaphysic is not confined to past ages. If for 'ordained of God' we substitute 'ordained by history', or 'the will of the German nation', or 'the spirit of France', or 'the true spirit of the Party', we can find plenty of recent and contemporary parallels. In contrast to this kind of metaphysic, egalitarians have tended—so far as their philosophical climate permitted—to be empirical in their approach. They have tried to remind people of the hard facts, sometimes in very simple ways, as in the line directed against the French aristocrats: *'Nous sommes hommes comme ils sont'.*

Since most establishments are usually propped up by some kind of false metaphysic, this appeal to facts has often succeeded. In the light of human similarities, hierarchies tend to appear arbitrary and irrational. There is a close and important parallel here with the tendency to question individual morality. Just as an adolescent, who has hitherto accepted the customary and traditional morality served up to him by

1. For this distinction see pp. 40–1
2. *Richard II*, Act III, Scene 2, lines 54–5.

his parents or other authorities, may find it arbitrary in the light of his reason and experience, so a society may emerge from the childhood phase of dependence on authority and question its traditional values: indeed, we might claim that the individual and social rebellion are casually connected. It is possible that history shows a trend towards a more liberal and humane attitude in relation to authority: but this trend, if indeed it exists, is not irreversible, and irrational tyrannies are always apt to break out, as in the classic case of Nazi Germany.

If there is such a trend it is certainly connected with the increased ability of the ego to understand and control reality: or, in less stilted language, with man's increased ability to grasp the laws of nature and deploy his reason upon his environment. As he does so, he lessens his dependence on the traditional hierarchy, and is less frightened of the possibilities of his own freedom. This is why the concepts of freedom, reason, and empirical understanding (chiefly in the form of science) have traditionally gone hand in hand with egalitarianism: and for the same reason the notion of the essential goodness of human nature has also played a large part. Thus Godwin says that 'government'— what we might call 'the super-ego' or 'the establishment'— 'prompts us to seek the public welfare, not in innovation and improvement, but in a timid reverence for the decisions of our ancestors, as if it were the nature of mind always to degenerate, never to advance'.

It is in some such sense as this, then, that we can oppose the egalitarian virtues to the 'establishment' virtues. Of course, both are important. Just as we need free enquiry, questioning of the established order, individual initiative, and the refusal to accept a position of inferiority, so also we need loyalty, law and order, security, and integration in our society. The two do not necessarily conflict, at least in theory: an excessively strict tyranny in a society may have results opposite to those which it endeavours to enforce, and end up in revolution and chaos; and conversely an excessively free democracy may find itself suddenly under the control of a tyrant. So too a man whose conscience is unduly severe may find himself a prey to a mental break-down or a compulsive act of passion; and a man insufficiently governed by conscience or an external set of rules may find his own desires more tyrannous and compulsive than any conscience could have been.

Whether there are any general principles governing the degree of egalitarianism permissible in any individual or society is a question we shall examine later.[1] Here we need to observe, in the light of what we have just said, the different functions which assertions about equality may perform in a historical context. These assertions have usually been made in situations in which people think that they or others are being wrongly treated, and in which they want something done about it. This is true of most political ideals. Women want to be emancipated, Negroes want to vote, working-class parents want their children to have a chance to be properly educated: and such demands are usually expressed in terms of 'liberty', 'equality', 'democracy', 'justice', and so forth. We could induce from this that these people simply *seized on* such ideals as a way of expressing their particular demands: but this account itself forbids us to induce that there are, as it were, no ideals to seize on. There is, of course, such a thing as using words like 'equality' as slogans, as a form of good publicity merely: much as words like 'undemocratic', 'un-English', or 'un-American' have been used without a great deal of descriptive content but just as terms of criticism or abuse. But the possibility of such a misuse itself suggests the possibility of a more proper use of these terms. However many cases there may be where people have cheated, there must be at least some cases where they have played fair. Thus these assertions are not often *merely* slogans or embodiments of specific protests. Behind the cry of 'Down with privilege!', or a particular objection to a particular privilege, lies the view that some things *really are* privileges while others are not: that men *have* certain natural characteristics (which are, on the whole, similar in all men) on the one hand, and are *given* certain powers, benefits, or social status on the other hand. It is appropriate to speak of privilege (*privilegium*, a 'private law' for the benefit of a particular individual or group) when the artificially granted status or power is not connected to or justified by any natural characteristics.

1. See pp. 165–8.

What natural characteristics justify what status, powers, or treatment may seem an open question: but in practice it is not treated as entirely open. It is doubtful whether many people have seriously believed that being born into an aristocratic or rich family, for instance, is in *itself* a justification for different treatment: and it is significant that historically such justification has always needed the support of some conjoined proposition, such as that certain characteristics which all recognise as desirable are passed by heredity from aristocrats to their sons. What has happened in history is not so much that we have changed our criteria of what empirical characteristics are relevant to powers and treatment, but rather that, by more assiduous attention to the facts, we have come to realise that certain empirical characteristics which we thought (or vaguely assumed) to have existed do not in fact exist. As soon as you cease to believe that an aristocrat is, in point of hard fact, significantly superior to other men, you can no longer seriously maintain that he ought to have more power or better treatment: it would be like maintaining that all those whose names began with the letter Q should be treated differently. Similarly, as soon as we learn from empirical tests that woman and Negroes have the same feelings and capacities as men and whites, we no longer feel justified in treating them as inferiors. Few people have held, as the result of serious rational reflection, that women should be treated as inferiors simply because of their physical difference from men: just as few people really hold that Negroes should be treated as inferiors *simply* because they are black. It is logically possible, perhaps, to hold this: but it is not common to do so.[1]

Demands for equality, then, although made with an eye to specific privileges, are not as specific in their meaning as we might suppose. They are, rather, reminders of criteria that we already have. These might be criteria which the authorities purport to be adopting already, but occasionally (through forgetfulness or deceitfulness) fail to live up to. The reminder then is like an accusation of cheating, but in a more general way. For example, if a government publicly professes the view that differences in wealth should not

[1]. For a more detailed discussion of this kind of reasoning see pp. 109 and following.

affect educational opportunity, but we find that government supporting a system (such as the public schools in England) which plainly favours the rich, we can make a simple accusation of cheating or dishonesty. But if the government, without committing itself to any view at all, supports this system we can accuse it of failing to *recognise* or *admit to* the generally accepted belief that wealth should not be relevant to education.

To describe such reminders as tautologies or platitudes may be legitimate, but must not be allowed to blind us to their function. To say '*Nous sommes hommes comme ils sont*', or 'Women are human beings too, you know' or 'The poor need educating as much as the rich', by reminding us of natural characteristics which are common to ordinary people as well as to aristocrats, males and the rich, thereby accuse the hearer of using some irrelevant characteristic to justify different treatment. 'This isn't a police state' would be used, in contemporary England, to imply that some authority was breaking an accepted rule, that he was not 'playing the game': rather as people used to say in England: 'That's not cricket', extending the game-metaphor into the field or moral and political rules.

2

Man and Nature

The dictionary definition quoted in the Introduction[1] makes a rough distinction between two kinds of equality. There is a difference between what we may call *natural* similarity ('identical in amount, magnitude . . .' etc.) and *artificial* or man-made similarity ('on the same level in dignity, power, excellence, etc.: having the same rights or privileges'). Two lines may be of equal length, or two men of equal weight: but these are simply facts which we note. The equality is not of our own choosing. On the other hand, two objects may be regarded as of equal value, or two men may have an equal voice in the government of a country: here we *treat* them as the same in a certain respect. We do not find them equal: *we count them as* equal.

This distinction is and always has been crucial for all egalitarian thinkers. For their case is, characteristically, that because men are equal in the first sense they ought therefore to be equal in the second: that is, the natural equality of men ought to be mirrored in an equality of status or treatment. But the concepts of 'nature' and 'human nature' are far more obscure than we might think: and what I have just represented as a single distinction between 'natural' and 'artificial' is actually no more than a mask that covers many different distinctions and many difficult problems. Of these I shall deal only with those which seem especially relevant to our main theme.

1. pp. 16–7.

a) Nature and Status

Perhaps the most obvious interpretation of the distinction suggested by the dictionary is that it rests not upon whether nature or man is responsible for a certain similarity but upon what kind of similarity it is. I could make a shorter line equal in length to a longer by adding to it, or a fatter man equal to a thinner by cutting slices off him: but the equality thereby produced would still be natural rather than artificial. I should have changed nature by my action, but the equality would still be *in* nature. We can contrast this with artificial equality by describing the latter as equality of *status*. People who are equals in this sense do not necessarily have anything in common except this status: and since status is a man-made thing, this sort of equality is wholly artificial. The notion of status, like the related notions of roles and rights, is only comprehensible in reference to a set of man-made rules and ordinances.

But it is far from clear on what the distinction between 'natural fact' and 'status' is really based. The difficulty here is that there is a sense in which even the most 'natural' similarities are of our own making. We can only call two things similar in virtue of some rule or criterion of similarity. Thus whether two objects are the same colour depends on what we count as 'the same colour'; and, in fact, different people might have different criteria (some people content themselves with the single category 'yellow', others talk about 'canary', 'muted lemon', and so on). The same holds of other simple 'natural' similarities: we can only talk of 'the same height' or 'the same weight' by reference to some standard of measurement. So 'natural' similarities seem to depend on a framework of rules just as much as do 'artificial' similarities. Moreover, these rules have to be learnt and taught: when a child learns to talk a large part of his task is to grasp certain criteria of similarity which adults use in language. Until he has done this he will be unable to make appropriate use of common nouns and adjectives—'lion', 'tree', 'man', 'round', 'heavy', etc.—since the whole point of these words is to denote recurrent similarities. We call one object a tree, and another object a tree, because they seem to us to be *like* each other.

If we now ask 'But are things which we count as similar

really similar?' it seems difficult to attach any sense to our question. Two red objects are certainly similar: but this means only that we classify them as similar by virtue of a public criterion which already exists in our language, and is expressed by the word 'red'. We cannot intelligibly ask 'Are they really red?': for it is only *within* the framework of the language that we can ask whether something is red or not, and to be within the framework is already to have learnt the criteria of redness. To invent new criteria of similarity would be, *pro tanto*, to invent a new language. This is certainly possible: young children who wish to classify certain things under a common heading often invent new criteria of classification in the form of new words. Thus children could invent a word 'scrawly' for anything which would take the mark of a crayon. What we call walls, ceilings, and table-mats, as well as pieces of paper, would be 'scrawlies'. Now we may be tempted to say that the similarity between scrawlies is real and not invented, since it can be explained and understood by people who do not use the word (as I have just explained it and you have understood it): that it is a similarity which anyone could simply *observe*. But it is not clear that we do 'simply observe' similarities in this way. We may observe two things that we afterwards classify as 'red': but we cannot know *that* they are both red without using the public criterion of redness, and to be able to use this criterion is to have learnt what 'red' means. So with all similarities: we need an independent check, which is in fact provided by a public language, to tell us that we are correct in counting two instances as similar.

Again, it is true that children react in the same way to circumstances that we count as similar. A child will stretch out its hands for one piece of chocolate, and stretch them out again for another similar piece: if I prick it with a pin twice it will cry on both occasions: and so on. But animals, and even inanimate objects, do this sort of thing also. We cannot say that the child has *recognised* that, or *knows* that, the two are similar unless it used some word or conventional sign correctly, such as saying 'Hurts!' when (and only when) we hurt it, as opposed to merely crying or shrieking; and even this might not be sufficient evidence.

The position can be more complicated than this, however.

Suppose I find a certain type of girl attractive, but not a type that can be adequately described by an existing word such as 'blonde', 'boyish', 'stately', etc. So I invent a word, and say that I like 'squiggly' girls. Have I not now observed a new similarity, and marked it with a private word of my own? Not quite. Suppose you ask me what 'squiggly' means, and I say 'Well, it's a combination of boyishness, and fair complexion, and swaying hips . . .' and so on. Then I have not really noted a new similarity: I am simply getting you to reshuffle similarities which we all recognise (being boyish, having a fair skin, etc.): and equally the word 'squiggly' is no longer really a private word of my own, since you now understand what it means. Now suppose I cannot explain what 'squiggly' means: not because I am stupid or bad at explaining, but because (as one might be tempted to say) 'there are no words for it'. Then how do I know there is such a thing as being squiggly? How do I know that I am not *making a mistake* on some of the occasions when I call girls squiggly? I can only know this by virtue of some public criterion of identification: and this means that 'squiggly' and its criteria cannot be entirely private.

Suppose, however, that you simply do not have the experiences that I have: could I then explain 'squiggly' to you? This is like asking whether we can teach a colour-blind person what 'purple' means. We can do so in the sense that we can teach him a translation (say 'a mixture of red and dark blue') and tell him what criteria of identification are used in the language of which 'purple' is a part: what he cannot do, of course, is actually to *use* these criteria in life as well as in language. He knows what 'red' means: but he cannot identify red objects, not at least by his eyesight alone. Thus although there will have to be some other people who have experiences of such a kind that I can teach them 'squiggly' (otherwise I can give the word no meaning, even to myself), it is plain that what criteria of similarity groups of people adopt will depend on their interests and their sense-organs. A blind man, or somebody who could see 'squiggly' girls but did not find them attractive, would have little use for 'squiggly': and it is conceivable that a Martian, with totally different interests and sense-data from ourselves, would have little use for most of our criteria.

Because of this the distinction between natural and artificial similarity can still be upheld. For though it is within our power to choose by altering our language what things we shall count as similar, it appears that to some extent our criteria are forced on us: so that we still feel inclined to say of some similarities that we *find* them in nature, rather than create them by our own decision. The factors which force us, or at least strongly impel us, are to be found in our own biological and physiological make-up, and in certain ends and purposes which are common to all men. Thus although the categories of colour are to some degree flexible, they are to a great extent imposed on us by our particular sense-organs; and although it may be logically possible to construct a language which made no distinction between lions and ant-eaters, yet we are virtually bound to do so: for lions eat people, whereas ant-eaters only eat ants, and it is characteristic of human beings that they wish to avoid being eaten. Thus our biological equipment, together with considerations of common utility and convenience, in effect compel us to adopt particular criteria of similarity. Things that are governed by these criteria are naturally similar: and though the child learns that criteria, we could hardly conceive him creating different criteria altogether, since his sense-organs and purposes are the same as our own.

Hence we can draw our distinction by reference to the method of verification for natural and artificial similarities. If we want to find out whether one stick of dynamite is as powerful as another we explode them both and see if they make equally big bangs and perhaps equally big holes in the ground. We simply use our eyes and ears. Certainly we have to know what 'powerful' means in this context, and we have to accept a rough standard of measurement for the noise of the bangs and the size of the holes: but this is hardly relevant. For we all have to learn a common language and accept some common standards of measurement in order to be able to make judgements at all. But if we want to know whether one politician is as powerful as another, or whether the bishop is as powerful as the knight in chess, we have to learn the rules of a *particular* game: the game of chess, or the political system of a particular society. There is a sense in which we find bangs and holes in nature, and in which we do not find politicians or chessmen. We learn 'bang' and 'hole' by using our ears and eyes, and listening to our parents: but we can only learn 'politician' or 'pawn' by learning a special set of rules, which are not just rules of language, as well as by making empirical observations.

However, what we have noticed about language and similarity presents the egalitarian with a difficulty. If he relies on natural similarities to support an argument that there should or should not be certain similarities of status he now appears to be relying on similarities which must, logically, be the product of language. He can certainly exclude the particular games or systems of various human societies that produce artificial similarities: but he cannot exclude the whole artificial game or system of language, for even natural similarity only makes sense within such a game or system. Since many systems of language are logically conceivable, the egalitarian seems necessarily to be arguing for one sort of language rather than another: or at least for one set of criteria of similarity rather than another. Apparently he can only do this by claiming that one set of criteria is *better* (more useful, convenient, or profitable) than another, in that it satisfies human ends and purposes more efficiently. The form of his argument has now changed. Originally it seemed as if he were quoting a hard fact, the fact of natural similarity, as a criterion for judging the merits of certain social systems: now it seems as if he has already made a judgement of value in choosing one criterion from many possible criteria.

Thus suppose that I am dictator and have the power to arrange a social system: suppose, further, that I claim that I simply do not possess the concept of pain, and never use any of the words which other people use to express this concept. I then arrange a system in which people are given no sort of rights or status which mirrors their natural similarity as pain-feelers: some people are allowed to torture others, and since I claim not to possess the concept of 'torture' I naturally regard this with complete indifference, just as I am indifferent if an avalanche crushes a tree. You then say to me: 'Hey, human beings are similar to each other in that they can feel pain, and trees can't: you must take account of this similarity in your social arrangements.' But I reply: 'There may be a criterion of similarity to that effect in your language, but why should I adopt your language? Whatever you may mean by "pain" and "torture", it doesn't concern me.' Then you may say: 'But if you don't take this criterion into account your social arrangements will be unfair': and now I reply: 'You are arguing in a circle. You seem to have decided what arrangements are fair, and are only persuading me to use this particular criterion because it happens to support these arrangements. I thought the existence of the criterion was supposed to *show* us what arrangements are fair; and as the criterion only exists in your language, not in mine, I don't see why I should take account of it.'

To this the egalitarian has three answers. First, he may say: 'Frankly, I do not believe that you do not yourself make use of this criterion. You really know quite well what the criterion is, and it is included in your own stock of criteria: you are just pretending.' Secondly, he may say: 'Even though you do not need this criterion yourself because you never feel pain, yet it is a genuine one, and makes a useful distinction. It enables us to predict things that you could not predict (such as screams, flight, fear, and so on) and hence it gives us increased control over reality. This is sufficient for you to admit its existence, and to learn it from us: if you like to put it so, let us say that our language is superior to yours in this respect.' Thirdly, he may say: 'Since your arrangements are made for people who do speak this language and make this distinction, they can only be fair if you take account of it: you have no right to say that your criteria are better than ours, and you must use the criteria of similarity used by those you are dealing with.'

All these answers are interesting, and each points to a different plank that the egalitarian may use for his platform. First, it is often the case that tyrants and dictators *pretend to forget*, or perhaps actually do forget, natural similarities which exist even within their own language, and criteria which are part of the common human heritage. The egalitarian has to jog their memory, or accuse them of dishonesty. Secondly, if we discover new similarities, or produce new criteria, the egalitarian can reasonably say that the authorities ought to attend to them. For if they are genuine they can be shown to give us more control and greater predictive powers, and this is universally accepted to be desirable—indeed we might say, putting it briefly, that our desire for control over the world is what underwrites the whole apparatus of language and empirical knowledge. Thirdly, the egalitarian wants to deny that one person can legitimately impose his criteria of his language on another. For if I make you note some similarities and neglect others I am, in effect, imposing my values on you: I am telling you that what is important in my language is really important, irrespective of what distinctions you make in yours. The egalitarian claims that I have no right to force this judgement of value on you: you may accept my criteria (perhaps for the reason given above, that they draw finer and hence more useful distinctions), but then you will be accepting them by virtue of your own criteria of what is important—namely, the drawing of finer and hence more useful distinctions—so that your acceptance will be voluntary and not forced. This is perhaps the most important point of the three, and I shall return to it in later chapters.[1]

We shall assume, then, that natural equality consists in similarities that can be verified by observation within the framework of a language in the way that we have described: whereas artificial equality, or equality of status, depends on some further set of rules, which have to be learnt if the similarities are to be understood. Though I hope that what I have said above has gone some way to clarifying the distinction theoretically, it is often difficult to draw in practice with reference to human characteristics in society.

For the capacity to imitate and to learn, and hence to engage in activities which are conventional or 'artificial' rather than 'natural'—activities which are governed by rules —is one of the most important differences between man and the animals. It connects very closely with the notions of intelligence, purpose, and will. Hence we may well find that what we took to be natural characteristics are actually artificial, not only in the sense that they are artificially created by the will of men working upon nature but in the more important sense that the characteristics only exist in reference to a set of human conventions: that is, they are not really natural characteristics at all, but social roles. We

1. See pp. 153–68.

might say that it is natural for human beings to have the *desire, need,* or *capacity* to be language-users, friends, husbands, citizens, etc.: but *to be* a language-user, friend, husband, or citizen is to take part in something artificial, in a game governed by rules. Again, an egalitarian might wish to argue that since women as well as men are rational (or are equal in being rational), therefore to treat them unequally (e.g. by keeping them in purdah, not allowing them to join clubs, vote, etc.) is wrong. But if we take 'being rational' to mean that women actually abide by the rules of a certain game—that they use logic rather than intuition, avoid *ad hominem* arguments, remain calm and unemotional during discussion, and so forth—then perhaps women are not equally rational. If the egalitarian had based his argument on the female *capacity* for abiding by the rules of the game (and 'being rational' might bear this sense) it might seem more plausible.

Let us see how the egalitarian is led into talk about rational capacities. There is a point in saying 'All men are born equal' which is not made by saying simply 'All men are equal'. The point is, of course, that there may be more similarities amongst human beings at birth than amongst human beings as adults. Some of the similarities and dissimilarities in adults may not be natural but man-made, i.e. produced by other human beings during the course of their upbringing and education. These similarities and dissimilarities would not be matters of status but matters of fact. But since they might nevertheless be *produced* by equality or inequality of status, it is plain that notions of natural and artificial equality, though logically distinguishable, bear a very close relationship in practice. For instance, two adults may be dissimilar in intelligence, as a result of environmental factors which are themselves the result of human rules and ordinances. Once we know what the factors are, the egalitarian will be inclined to say that the men were naturally equal in intelligence, but had been made unequal.

But how far can we retreat in this way? Suppose we discovered that dissimilarities were produced pre-natally, in embryos, by different types of behaviour on the part of the mother: and suppose further that some of this behaviour at least was controlled by our own artificial rules, whether political or social. Then some children will be born who are dissimilar to others: and this dissimilarity would be accounted for by the fact, say, that their mothers had to work during pregnancy, whereas richer mothers did not. Can we now say that the newly born children were naturally equal, but have been made unequal? It seems reasonable to say this, because we assume a continuity between the embryo and the child: but if we wished to include these particular similarities in our statement 'All men are equal' we should have to count embryos as men, which is slightly odd. If we do not give way at this point we should certainly have to give way if the case were pushed further. Suppose now that dissimilarities appear in embryos which were not due to any differences in the original male and female chromosomes but to certain conditions during copulation or conception. It now becomes absurd to attribute any natural equality to men in respect of the characteristics in which the embryos are dissimilar. Embryos may count as men, but not chromosomes.

It is important to note, however, that whatever date we take as our starting-point for the existence of a human being, we are unlikely to remain totally uninterested in what leads up to that existence, in what we may call the prehistory of the person. In so far as we become, as we are rapidly becoming, able to control that prehistory in such a way as to make an important difference to the ultimate human product, we shall probably want to argue about the rules whereby that control is exercised. We shall call some fair and just and others unfair and unjust: and in such a situation it would not be irrelevant or absurd to stress the similarities of embryos or even chromosomes. 'All embryos are equal' may sound silly as a piece of political theory, but if a man's happiness depends on what happens to—shall we say 'him' or 'his embryo'?—prenatally, then it would have a great deal of point.

As our powers over nature increase, we are bound to become less interested in what men are, and more interested in what we make them to be. The importance of asserting natural similarities amongst men depends to some extent on our lack of control over these similarities: they are brute facts to which politicians and others should attend. Once we achieve control over them, our interest focusses on whatever moral or political principles we think should be used in the course of this control. But this is now no longer a matter of what we have called natural equality: that is, the respects in which all men are equal as a matter of empirical fact; we are concerned rather with artificial equality, with what rules should be set up for altering and controlling the facts.

The egalitarian may well want to stake most of his money on equality of capacity, rather than on an apparently ever-decreasing number of 'natural' similarities. But what a man is or could be, what he does or could do, and hence the ways in which his qualities or performances are or could be equal to those of others, depends on what counts as a man. In practice we usually have a fairly clear picture by reference to which we settle such questions. But it is important to realise that the central point does not lie in our having clear logical criteria for 'man' either now or in the future. The real difficulty is that, as our power over human nature increases, it becomes less and less intelligible to talk about 'human nature' at all. Even today it is reasonably plain that what we call 'natural capacities', such as the capacity for being virtuous, or determined, or intellectually curious, are the result of upbringing and education. If and when we reach the stage, which still sounds at present somewhat fantastic, of being able to influence and create capacities and abilities to an infinite degree, what sense will we be able to give to such a phrase as 'natural capacity'?

So long as were able to identify the *bearer* of 'natural capacity' (even if this bearer were what we should now call a set of genes or chromosomes, rather than what we now call a human being), there would still be a sense for the phrase: and this is only to say that we would still know what we were talking *about*. By the 'natural capacities' of a thing we shall mean, roughly, what the thing could do, be, or become. Now there are no absolute logical limitations on the doing, being or becoming of anything in the world. Pigs might fly, might be lighter than air, and might become aeroplanes: just as now tadpoles can swim, can be more than an inch long, and can become frogs. But in practice two considerations delimit our use of 'natural capacity'. First, there are practical limitations on what things can do, be, or become, with or without the help of human skill. Pigs cannot fly, and we cannot give every child the I.Q. of a genius. Second, most of the things in which we are interested, as ordinary people rather than as scientists, retain a fairly constant identity. There are exceptions: water can become ice, and tadpoles frogs. But pigs and human beings are less mobile, and cannot easily become other things besides themselves.

Hence we may, perhaps rather arbitrarily, define a natural capacity as what a thing can *in practice* do, be, or become, whilst remaining itself. This is an essential move if we are not to reduce to nonsense the egalitarian notion of making society reflect natural similarities and capacities. For we might argue: 'Given sufficient techniques, we can make anything we like out of man. Therefore man has no natural capacities at all: or, if you prefer, he has the natural capacity to be anything we choose. Therefore when egalitarians say that the natural capacities of people are equal, this is only trivially true, in the sense that there are no limits to what any person can become: and when they say that society ought to develop men's natural capacities they must mean that we ought to make the best of everybody, which again is true but exceedingly obvious.' This is fair argument, but our two practical delimitations still allow the egalitarian sufficient scope. For, first, we do not have these techniques: and it is doubtful whether the practical limits on what we can (in practice) make people can ever extend as far as the logical limits on what they can (in theory) become. And, secondly, if (as is likely) we restrict our interests to what *a man* can become without changing into some other entity, then we thereby restrict ourselves to certain capacities only, namely those that could reasonably be described as human.

b) *The Deification of Nature*

There are a great many other uses of 'natural' which we have not space to consider here. But there is one distinction which needs to be made firmly: for although it is a very simple one, failure to observe it is still responsible for a great deal of very dangerous thinking.

This is simply the distinction between (1) 'natural' in its descriptive uses (including those already discussed), and (2)

'natural' as a prescriptive or evaluative term. 'Normal' shows
the same ambiguity. Either it just means 'average', 'ordinary',
'to be expected', or 'in the common run of things': or it
means 'healthy', 'proper', 'desirable', or 'to be approved'.
Sometimes (3) words like 'natural' and 'unnatural', 'normal'
and 'abnormal', are used with both meanings at once: and
it is essential to be clear whether the speaker intends a value-
judgement or not. Thus in 'unnatural practices', as applied
to homosexuality or some other kind of sexual behaviour,
'unnatural' may mean (1) 'out of the ordinary' or 'uncom-
mon': (2) 'wrong', 'wicked', or 'immoral': or (3) both at
once.

Thus somebody might say 'Homosexuality is wrong because it's unnatural'. But as it stands this does not seem a
very good argument. If by 'unnatural' he means (1) that
homosexuality is a minority phenomenon, it cannot be a
good argument: for there are plenty of minority phenomena
which we consider desirable, such as extreme saintliness or
heroism: and, in general, why should unusual things be
wrong? If he means (2) that homosexuality is wrong or
immoral, it cannot be an argument at all: for he has only
succeeded in saying 'Homosexuality is wrong because it's
wrong'. (The same applies if he means (3) both that it is a
minority phenomenon and that it is wrong.)

It is a psychological curiosity that many people would
still feel themselves to be somehow cheated out of their beliefs by this analysis. Things like homosexuality, incest, parri-
cide, and many others, they might wish to say, are somehow
really unnatural: they do not want to say *merely* that
they are unusual, or *merely* that they are wrong, but that
they are in some sense not 'in accordance with nature', and
hence *necessarily* wrong. To make sense of this we would
have to represent Nature—and for this purpose it should have
a capital N—as some kind of person, or law-giver, or moral
arbiter. Such a picture makes the best sense of phrases like
'natural law', 'Nature intends us to . . .' 'Human beings are
naturally designed for . . .', or even such harmless-sounding
phrases as 'The natural place of woman is . . .' or 'The purpose
of sex is . . .' or 'Men are meant to . . .' The archetype of this
way of talking is, of course, belief in a God who controls
Nature and issues edicts in the light of which certain

behaviour is 'natural' in the sense of 'right' or 'commendable' as well as in other senses.

It is important to see that a metaphysic of this kind, whether it be intelligible or unintelligible, true or false, does not help us to establish human equality as a natural fact. Many people have phrased their belief in basic or ultimate human equality in some such terms as 'equal in God's sight'. (They may prefer to speak in terms of Providence, or the Spirit of the Universe, or Nature, but these differences are not relevant in the present context.) Let us suppose that they mean that God has no favourites but values or treats us all equally. This would be an assertion of fact; and an important one, if we assume that there is a God, and that how he treats or values us makes an important difference to human life on earth. It would be important in the same way as it would be important for animals in the zoo to know that the keeper valued them all equally and gave them equal treatment: or as it is important to children to know that their father loves them all equally. Yet this would be asserting a different kind of equality from a natural equality based on a number of shared human characteristics. A father may love all his children equally, without there being any empirical characteristic common to them all.

In order to believe that this equality in the eyes of God was relevant to how we should treat each other, we should have to bring in another assertion: the assertion that the way God values or treats us, i.e. equally, is the *right* way. It is quite possible to believe in a God of whose moral values one disapproves. There is a vast difference between (a) believing in a God or super-being who imposes on us a system of natural laws, natural rights, and natural obligations, and who counts us as equal, and (b) believing in a God who does all this *and whom we ought to obey*. The whole network of natural law and natural rights, within which the notion of natural equality historically grew up, is based on this religious view: and to do justice to the idea of equality 'in the sight of God' it might be thought necessary to consider the whole view at some length. But we are in some degree excused from such a discussion by the distinction just mentioned. Briefly, we believe (a) simply as a matter of fact, just as we can believe that the laws and legal rights current in England are such-and-such, without making any moral judgement about whether they are good laws or moral rights: but we can only believe (b), that we ought to fall in with God's system, on the basis of some moral judgement of our own: just as to say that we ought to obey an English law is to make a moral judgement. The mere existence of the law, or any facts about it, does not suffice for (b): and similarly the facts that a God created us, watches over us, punishes us, loves us, and so on, however important, are not a complete reason for falling in with his edicts, or for adopting his point of view.

It follows that the same arguments can be advanced, in this context at least at a purely human level as are advanced on the level of supernatural metaphysics. For instance, we might discuss whether retributive punishment is a good thing. If we believe in a God or super-being, who is not necessarily good or wise, then it simply does not matter whether this God himself punishes people or not, or whether he approves or disapproves of such punishment. But if we believe in a good God, then part of what we mean in calling him good is that he satisfies our own moral criteria; and then the question 'Does God (who is necessarily good) believe in retributive punishment?' virtually turns into the question 'Is retributive punishment good?' Thus if we decide (as, on the whole, Christians have come to believe during this century) that retributive punishment is not as good as we thought, then what happens is that we change our conception of the will of God: and, in fact, sophisticated Christians now tend to believe in a God whose views do not favour retributive punishment (or anyway not much). The *moral* authority of a God (as of any other authority, such as a sacred scripture or a church) can only come from our own moral decisions.

This is not to say that the whole notion of authority is useless; those who deny all force or truth to religion may still accept certain people or certain writings as valuable for morality. But the specific arguments which we may have about equality, or any other moral issue, do not have to be conducted in religious terms: and this gives us hope that the considerations advanced in this book are just as relevant to those of a religious persuasion as to those of none. It is possible that religious belief may *add to* moral arguments of this kind: but the arguments will not *miss the point* even if they do not take a specifically religious form.

All these uses of 'natural' overlook, and indeed tacitly deny, what we have seen to be at least one of the most important distinctions between 'man' and 'nature': namely that man makes and follows his own rules, possesses the powers of intention, deliberation, and choice, and creates his own values, whereas in nature—to put it crudely—things just happen. There is all the difference in the world between an intentional human action on the one hand, and something that happens to a man or that he does unwittingly or accidentally on the other. In the latter case he is not really *acting*: he is simply a physical object in space and time that *reacts* to its environment. There is thus an important sense in which man, *qua* man, is not a natural phenomenon at all, but rather acts on nature: in which there is, to put it paradoxically, no such thing as human nature, but simply a man's powers of deliberation and choice operating on a natural world, which includes his own mind and his own body just as it includes more remote phenomena. This is not to say, of course, that these powers are magical or unpredictable, or that they are not causally connected with those mental and physical phenomena which we can quite properly lump together as 'human nature' or count as part of what we mean by 'a man'. But the logical and practical differences between the powers and the phenomena on which they operate are extremely important.

It is the failure to see, or perhaps to tolerate psychologically, this truth that leads us into the temptations described above. Crushed by the burden of choice, or the difficulties of achieving real freedom in making our moral and political decisions, we try to get 'nature' (or some kind of 'super-nature', perhaps in the form of a God) to do our work for us. This is usually done in one of two ways. Thus on the one hand it was possible for Rousseau to believe in the noble savage and for Wordsworth to hold that children come into this world trailing clouds of glory. For them the burden of freedom was light, because man was naturally good and had only to be his true self in order to remain good. On the other hand the more tough-minded and pessimistic thinkers, such as Hobbes and Schopenhauer, whose pictures of human nature are considerably grimmer, lighten the burden either by denying the existence of any real freedom at all or by persuading us to abandon it.

We have to avoid the temptation to regard 'nature' as either angelic or diabolical: but it does not follow from this that nature is *irrelevant* to our moral and political choices. Indeed, it is the only thing we have on which to base them. To turn away from the facts, or to be reluctant in being guided by them, suggests a hostility to nature which is as doctrinaire as any other *a priori* approach. This is simply to say that we need facts rather than myths: and we have to remember that facts about human beings come not from those pictures which happen to please us, but from the work of biologists, psychologists, sociologists, and others, whose method at least approximates to the scientific. I stress this point here because the scope of this book does not allow us to examine in detail any of the particular facts about 'human nature' on which egalitarians or their opponents might wish to rely. But as a point of methodology it has to be continually borne in mind. Nobody who takes morality or politics seriously can afford to disregard those disciplines which relate to 'human nature'. For even though they have not reached their maturity as sciences, the mere attempt to follow them as disciplines will help to prevent us lapsing into one of the almost infinite number of myths about 'human nature': myths which in this century have lost some of their crudity but none of their currency.

3

Is there an Absolute
Principle of Equality?

We have seen what sort of sense can be attached to the concept of a natural human characteristic: and we saw earlier that historical demands for equality were attempts to change the rules of the game *in a particular way*: namely, by rearranging the rules so that status, powers, and treatment are more justifiable than before, in the light of those natural characteristics of human beings that we think to be relevant. But which are these? Is it possible to have a hard-and-fast set of criteria which will allow us to state unequivocally that 'more equality' or 'absolute equality' has been achieved?

Suppose we are playing bridge, which is almost entirely a game of skill. We can say that all the players are equal under the rules: that is, the rules apply to all. But somebody who had a very poor memory, or was otherwise deficient in the skill required for bridge, might complain of inequality or unfairness, since because of his deficiency he might always lose the game and his money. So we change the game to poker or pontoon, where different skills are required. But then somebody also complains: someone who perhaps had a good memory and all the skills needed for bridge but who was bad at keeping a poker face and hence always lost at poker. We get fed up and turn to something quite new, like a guessing game or a game of tennis: but the same thing happens. Whatever game we play it is bound to favour some people and handicap others, because success in every game depends on some natural characteristic, such as a good memory or the ability to guess well.

Thus it may seem that no one game gives us 'more equality'

than another: the only equality we can hope for is that which must, logically, occur in all games, namely an impartial application of the rules. The only way out of this seems to be to make the game into one of pure chance, like roulette or bingo. Here there could be said to be 'absolute equality', because the natural characteristics of the players—their skills and talents—do not count at all. We could also say, perhaps, that we 'increased equality' the more we approached a game of chance. This way out is important, and we shall come back to it later: but the objection to it is plain—it gives all the players equal treatment, but it does not give them equal powers or equal scope, since it does not give them any powers or scope at all. They just sit there, and win or lose by pure chance. Since people commonly like to deploy their skills and talents, some other solution seems desirable.

Here, however, the game-metaphor has misled us. It is common to all games that only certain characteristics of the players count. Their skills, talents, intelligence, farsightedness, and so on count: but their birth, wealth, and social status do not count. But this is not true of most social systems: and to this extent they are radically unlike anything that could properly be called a game. There are indeed activities or pastimes in which individuals are rewarded if they can produce certain objects from their pockets, or are wearing certain articles of clothing, and these might be called games. But they would have to be objects and articles that all the players might reasonably be expected to have or wear. It would be tolerable to give a prize to the first man on the dance-floor to produce a penknife or show that he is wearing suspenders: but intolerable to reward the man with the bluest blood, or the man who can produce a valid cheque for £100,000

We can say, then, that equality is 'increased' or a state of 'absolute equality' approached as we progressively remove *accidental* features, and concentrate more and more on natural features that all men might be reasonably expected to have, at least in some degree. The demand for equality then appears as a demand that society should be conducted more like a game, and less like a purely artificial device which favoured certain groups whose natural characteristics were in no way different from those of other people. This goes some way towards meeting the case: but it still does not meet our first point, that since people's talents and skills are different there are bound to be some permanent losers, whatever system of rules we adopt and whatever game we play.

a) Equality of Opportunity

This is the difficulty which also confronts the notion of equality or opportunity: and we may make some progress by a specific consideration of this notion. There is a sense in which all the players in a game have an equal opportunity of winning: that is, the rules do not favour one more than another. But unless the game is a game of pure chance, we might also say that in fact some players have a better chance or more opportunity to win than others, if they have superior skills or talents. So we are not sure whether to say that they all really have an equal opportunity or not.

Thus if, when we say 'Every American boy has the same opportunity to be President', we mean simply that there are no rules which disqualify him *a priori* (because he is poor, or ugly, or the devotee of some minority religion), then this may be cold comfort: for in practice anyone who runs for the Presidency may need not only natural talents, like political ability and intelligence, but also perhaps accidental qualifications like wealth or social standing. Again, is it really true that everyone in England has an equal opportunity to go to a university when some people are too stupid to gain the necessary qualifications? We have replaced the criterion of wealth by the criterion of intelligence, but the actual opportunities seem no more equal than before—hitherto we had a group of poor people who were in this respect underprivileged, and now we have a group of stupid people who are underprivileged. We have simply changed the rules.

Suppose, however, we adopt a different criterion from wealth or intelligence, the criterion of effort; and grant some privilege (such as university education) purely on this criterion. We should be inclined to say, I think, that we had approached more nearly to the principle of equality. This is because making an effort (we suppose) is something within the capacity of everyone, whereas being born into a rich family or being intelligent is not. By excluding wealth we have excluded accidental characteristics: and by excluding intelligence we distinguish between one kind of natural characteristics, those we *cannot help* having or not having, and another kind which we believe to be universally available —the capacity to make an effort, or to be kind, or some other capacity which is within the control of our will.

We have to suppose this in order to make sense of the notion of an equal opportunity, or of an equal chance. I may have the *right* to do things which I have not the power to do (stupid people have the right to go to a university), or be *entitled* to do them, for these words refer simply to the rules of the game. But if I have not the power, then strictly speaking I do not have the opportunity or the chance. The door of the cell may be unlocked and the warder absent, but I do not have the opportunity or chance to escape if I am crippled or paralysed. We could say that I had the chance if at that particular time I was asleep, but in this case I still have the power to escape—it is just that I could not use the power at that moment. In one sense of 'could' it is false to say 'I had the opportunity, but I couldn't take it'; we usually mean that, no doubt for excellent reasons, I chose not to take it. ('I had the chance of a job in London, but I couldn't take it because my wife is ill and we have to live in Switzerland.' I am not really *compelled* to live in Switzerland: I merely think staying with my wife more important than getting a job in London.)

This analysis is by no means a full one, but it may at least help us to realise the various ways in which we are apt to disguise inequalities under the mask of the single word 'can'. 'Any American child *can* be President': this is true if it refers to rights or entitlements, false if it refers to opportunities or powers or capacities. Different uses of 'can' refer to different factors that allow us to do things or prevent us from doing them: these may take the form of rules and entitlements ('the king in chess can move one space in any direction'), permissions ('you can go, I've finished with you'), opportunities ('nobody's looking, we can escape now'), capacities for the future ('he can become the finest player in the world if he practises hard enough'), and abilities ('he can speak French'), besides various others that we might wish to distinguish.

It is sufficient for the present purpose to distinguish between things which people are actually able to do, either at once or within a reasonable space of time, and things that they are not able to do. For instance, a stupid person might never be able to gain the qualifications necessary for university entrance, or only be able to gain them if he worked very hard for fifty years. In the first case he simply does not have the capacity at all: in the second, we might by stretching a point say that he had the capacity, but the length of time is unreasonable, and in most contexts (if he were in his last year at school, for instance) we should probably say that he did not have it. How far we are prepared to stretch points in this way is to some degree an arbitrary matter, and depends on the context.

There are, however, some things which all or nearly all human beings are always or nearly always able to do: such things as making an effort, trying, using determination, and so on. It might be argued that it is for doing or not doing these things, in ways of which we approve or disapprove, that we punish and reward people, and distribute praise and blame: that these are things within the control of every man's will. Certainly there is a tendency for egalitarians to frame the rules of the game so that only these things count. If—and this is a big 'if'—all men share these abilities to an equal degree such a game would offer some hope of an absolute principle of equality.

Thus suppose we are organising a race for children of different ages and physiques. We might make them all start on the same line: but this would be unfair, because some are older and bigger than others. We then handicap them; and if we take enough characteristics into account in our handicaps—not only their size, but their known proficiencies at running fast, having stamina, being quick off the mark, and so on—then the effect of our handicaps is that, provided that they all make the same effort, they should all breast the tape at the same time. Of course, this never, or rarely, happens: but what we seem to be doing is to set up the rules so that only things like determination or the will to win count. We adjust all the characteristics that the children cannot do anything about, such as their size or the length of their legs, by handicapping them: and we leave only the things they can do something about, by applying determination or courage or some other moral quality.

But though the egalitarian tendency to set up games of this kind is noteworthy, it will not suffice for our present purpose. We can certainly define a class of moral characteristics or abilities or performances—the things we can do 'if we try' or 'if we choose', or 'if we make an effort'—and distinguish these from other characteristics which we cannot help having or not having. But if what we call 'determination', 'making an effort', 'courage', etc., are capacities which vary in degree from man to man, then there seems to be a sense in which it is as unfair to reward the determined and courageous as it is to reward the wealthy and intelligent.

It is important to see exactly why the idea that there are some things that everybody can do, and can do equally well, is necessarily false. The model case of asking whether I can do something is when I desire something, set myself to achieve it, and wonder whether I have the ability (power, entitlement, right, etc.) to achieve it. 'Can' here refers to the *implementation* of desires and wills: it is always a question of whether I can *do* something. That is why it makes little sense to ask whether somebody 'can want' or 'can will' something, for wanting and willing are not actions. To say that a person 'cannot want' to do something is not nonsense: but all we would mean is that, because of certain external factors, it is not to be conceived that he will, in fact, want to do it. A completely indoctrinated person 'cannot want' to disobey the Party: but to say this is just to say that he never will want to, because somebody has tampered with part of what the man is (his desires), not with any of the tools he uses to implement his desires by way of *action* (his abilities).

For the same reason it is odd to say 'I can't intend', or 'I can't try', or 'I can't decide'; for these words usually refer, not to what people do, but to states of mind that they find themselves in (like the state of wanting or desiring). It is not absurd to say these things, because the words may be used to refer to specific actions or results I wish to bring about.

Thus a neurotic may sensibly say 'I can't decide'; but here he represents coming to some decision—any decision—as a goal to be achieved in itself. It is not the respective merits of one or another course of action that worries him, but the difficulty of coming to a decision at all. We can say, if we like, that the general powers of trying, intending and deciding are powers which all human beings (unless they are totally mad) have: but the ability to make specific efforts, form specific intentions, or come to a decision in specific cases, varies from one man to another and from case to case, depending on the empirical facts. But it would be better to say simply that these 'general powers' are not really powers at all, but permanent states in which human beings find themselves.

How far a man can do things, how far he can implement his desires, is plainly a matter of empirical fact. Some of the tools he uses are whatever techniques are available to him in the outside world, but some are features which we are accustomed to regard as forming part of his personality, because in all normal people they do form such a part. These are things like determination, will-power, and effort: and a man may draw on these in exactly the same (logical) way as he draws on his physical resources, or uses external tools. If the resources are insufficient he cannot implement his desires: his tools are not good enough: he does not really have the chance. Since one man's tools are different from others' there is nothing that everybody can do equally well, in any serious sense.

This does not mean that the notion of 'equality of opportunity' is a completely incoherent one. We have seen that egalitarians prefer to change existing games and systems in a particular direction: roughly, away from those that favour external or 'accidental' attributes, towards those that favour natural characteristics which are 'part of the real self', as we might be tempted to say. To make all games dependent on moral effort seems to be the last item in this egalitarian programme. We can, as it were, go no further into the man's self: there are no more characteristics or attributes 'outside' him that we can strip away: we have arrived at the core. Now this programme can be represented as deriving from a certain picture of the self, or of what a man 'really is'. According to the picture, a man 'really is' his moral qualities: other attributes, such as intelligence, and still more his wealth or position in society, are not really 'him': they are things that 'he' has. In saying of every man that 'he' ought to have an equal opportunity, 'he' is intended in this sense: and if we accept this sense, we thereby accept that the egalitarian programme is desirable, for it is a programme specifically designed to fit this sense of 'he'.

In other words, the question of whether one game or system gives a person more equality of opportunity than another game or system depends ultimately on what we count as a person. The egalitarian adopts a narrow picture, whereby a person *is* determined and courageous, but only *has* intelligence, wealth, and a title. But this picture is not compulsory: we might alternatively say that a person is determined, courageous and intelligent, and *has* wealth and a title—or even that he *is* determined, courageous, intelligent, rich and aristocratic. Or we could outdo the egalitarian and say that he *has* determination and courage rather than that he *is* determined and courageous. So far as logic and language go, it seems arbitrary which picture we choose to adopt.

b) *Equality and Justice*

Yet there may be practical reasons why we adopt one picture rather than another, in particular contexts. If we are interested in the reward of merit we need a picture of the self which excludes characteristics which do not count as merits. We may thus feel inclined to interpret equality not as an absolute principle, but as a principle subordinate to justice of fairness. The real point of setting up such games, it seems, is not to put everyone on an equal footing, for in any absolute sense this appears to be logically impossible except in games of pure chance: it is rather to arrange things so that merit and desert are rewarded, rather than qualities which the individual can do nothing about. We are anxious to strip away all the non-moral characteristics, and leave only the moral ones, so that we can be sure of rewarding the right people.

Equality might enter into justice in two ways. First, it is a widely held principle of retributive justice that the reward should in some sense be equal to the merit, and that we should exact an eye for an eye and a tooth for a tooth. If I steal someone's car on Monday, he steals mine on Tuesday: and if I lend him my car on Wednesday, he lends me his on Thursday. That is simple retribution. The position may be more complicated: but equality is still operative as a principle. I may steal £50, and have to go to prison for three years: and we would justify this by believing that the punishment somehow equalled the crime, so that a state of imbalance was redressed and I would, as we say, have 'paid off my debt to society'. It would be unjust if I paid either more or less than my debt: I am supposed to repay an equal amount. Of course it is, strictly, impossible to measure the stealing of £50 against three years in prison; but we do nevertheless make some rough assessment. To send me to prison for life or hang me would be too severe, and to let me off with a caution not severe enough.

This must be distinguished from distributive justice, where we compare the cases of different individuals with each other. If you and I both steal £50, but you get off with a caution and I get sent to prison, this is unfair because our punishments are unequal, even though our crimes are the same. Similarly if I work a forty-hour week and put my back into it, while you sit at home and slack, it would be unfair if we both received the same amount of money. Equal merits and demerits, by this principle, ought to be equally rewarded or punished.

The difficulty here is that demands for equality seem, at first sight, to rely upon other principles besides desert or merit. An egalitarian would hold that if everyone has an equal need of food then everyone should have an equal right to it: and that however undeserving a man might be there are still some respects in which his treatment should be the same as other men—he should not be made a slave, or starved, or refused medical attention, just because he lacks merit. Indeed, it is usually egalitarians and liberals in general that oppose the notion of treatment according to merit or desert, and stress the importance of need.

But the notion of desert extends further than might be supposed. We think that those who suffer from some permanent handicap or misfortune, such as spastic children or

c

cripples, ought to be compensated for their handicaps by being given special attention. We could also quite reasonably say that they *deserve* it. Again, take the case of a child who is about to die from some incurable disease: we should naturally say that it was 'only fair' that what remained of his life should be made as happy as possible: and here it seems more natural to say that he deserved to have a better time than other children, rather than that he needed to. In this instance it almost seems as if the notion of justice is subordinate to the notion of equality, rather than vice versa: for in compensating the unfortunate we have in mind a level of happiness below which nobody should be allowed to fall. It is as if human beings all had an equal right to be happy, and if fate (in the form of disease, or a poor biological inheritance, or whatever) deals them an undeserved blow, it is our duty to make it up to them in some way.

But has it got to be an *undeserved* blow? Nobody can help being born a cripple or contracting an incurable disease: and when we say that destiny has not played fair with such a person we imply that it would have played fair if they had deserved it. They cannot have, since desert normally implies some kind of moral merit or demerit, which in these cases is lacking. There may, however, be things which we regard as so terrible or so wonderful that nobody could deserve them: however wickedly a man acts, we do not think that he deserves to be kept in prison and tortured for the whole of his life, and, however virtuous he is, we do not suppose that he deserves every single thing that any man might wish. Our opinion on whether there is an equal balance between wickedness and bad treatment (or between virtue and good treatment) may vary: but we always suppose that the balance should exist. Thus to those of a less sentimental age it might have seemed that some lazy rogue deserved to get no medical attention when he was ill, if he had been too lazy to make enough money to pay for it: but to us the spectacle of a man in pain without such attention is too unpleasant to be regarded as a punishment that does no more than equal his failings. We might even be prepared to put this positively and say that he deserved attention (rather than that he does not deserve to lack attention). This would be to suggest that there are some things which human beings deserve, simply by virtue of their being human, and irrespective of their moral merits.

That this is so can be seen by reverting to the case of those handicapped from birth. We should, surely, still feel that they deserved special benefits even if they were nasty, malicious, and generally vicious. It appears from this that we can use words 'deserve' and 'merit' even when a person, like the vicious-minded spastic or the lazy rogue who is ill, has nothing that we could reasonably describe as *a merit*. What people deserve, and what it is just or fair to give them, extends further than the notion of *moral* retribution, if by that we understand that those who are morally bad should get bad treatment, and those who are morally good should be treated well.

The notion of requital or compensation, on the other hand, is very much in place: which suggests that it is this notion that underlines the whole concept of justice. Even retribution is perhaps no more than a special case of this general principle of levelling or making equal. Criminals, and wicked people generally, *get away* with something which is nice for *them* but against the rules: they are, as it were, unfairly one up. By punishing them we equalise the score. Conversely, virtuous and talented people *give away* something which is nice for *us*, and may sometimes cost them an effort. They do more than their fair share, like those who perform works of supererogation: so it must be made up to them in the form of a reward. The criminal is like somebody who unfairly takes two turns running in a game: when we 'punish' him by ensuring that he misses his turn next time round, our object is not necessarily to exact vengeance, but simply to equalise the situation. Similarly the virtuous person who voluntarily forgoes his turn ought to be compensated by being given an extra turn next time.

This again suggests that the notion of equality or equalisation underlies the notion of justice or fairness; and certainly an egalitarian might want to hold that justice should be restricted to a process of compensation. There are, however, cases of justice where this seems not to be so, and it is important to see how the egalitarian would deal with these. Suppose I am by nature very strong and clever, so that the work I do is of great benefit to society, even though I may not do very much of it. Then many people would say it was just that I should get more money than other people not so strong or clever, even if they worked harder. Plainly this is because their criteria for desert are framed in terms of benefit to society, rather than in terms of moral effort. Of course, it is quite possible to frame any criteria for desert one wishes—to count anything as a merit: we could agree to reward the beautiful, or the bright-eyed, or the blue-blooded. But the egalitarian would object to rewarding these, and also to rewarding the strong and clever, either because these are characteristics outside the control of the individuals who possess them, or because it does not *cost* the strong and clever anything to exercise their strength and cleverness. He might in practice agree to reward the clever, perhaps on the utilitarian grounds that if you do not, the clever will stop working altogether or do the absolute minimum: but he would not agree on grounds of justice.

On the other hand he would perhaps agree to reward the conscientious and hard-working: not only on the utilitarian grounds that this would encourage others to be conscientious and hard-working, but also on grounds of justice. It *costs* a man something to be conscientious; in a sense he *does himself down*, and we have to equalise the situation by a reward. From this point of view it makes no signficant difference whether the man does himself down, or (like the spastic) is done down by fate. Suppose the player who takes two turns running does not in fact benefit by it, but rather brings disaster on himself, we should not necessarily want to make him lose his turn next time. Similarly if virtue is really its own reward, and if doing good to others costs us nothing, then we should doubt whether it was *just* to reward the virtuous: though it might still be expedient. In practice, we have to encourage people to behave virtuously and to work hard precisely because it does not, in itself, pay to do these things: and we have to discourage crime artificially, because 'crime does not pay' only if the criminal is caught and punished—if he is not, it pays very well. Sages from Plato onwards have tried to show that virtue is profitable and vice unprofitable in themselves: but this particular moral inoculation does not seem to have taken.

A game or social system in which moral effort, and only moral effort, was rewarded or compensated for might accord with the egalitarian view of justice. If we take the view that non-moral characteristics like intelligence or strength should not be rewarded, *either* because of the injustice of rewarding qualities beyond the individual's control, *and/or* because of the injustice of rewarding qualities which do not cost their owners anything to use, then we shall confine ourselves to games of exertion and moral effort only. But if we go further, and claim that some people are naturally better at making a moral effort than others (just as some are naturally stronger than others), then we might feel inclined to give up the idea that justice has anything to do with rewarding moral effort. It seems no more just to reward a person who is born conscientious than to reward a person who is born strong.

Throughout this discussion, however, we have been assuming that we are dealing with some power or capacity (like conscientiousness) which can vary in strength from man to man, due perhaps to circumstances outside the individual's control. If we were out to reward the *degree to which* such a power functioned—*how much* exertion or will-power the individual showed—then we might well call such a reward unfair. But we need here a distinction between absolute and relative capacities. We may be out to reward the *direction in which* a capacity like determination or will-power is used—whether the individual uses his will-power, however much or little he has, *for good or bad*. This capacity, the capacity for *directing* the will, is absolute rather than relative, in that we could not intelligibly say that one conscious being possessed more of it than another. Either you have it or you do not. In this sense, as we shall see,[1] it is a capacity which human beings all have—a capacity in respect of which they are equal or equals.

Some might still regard it as unjustifiable to reward and punish even the direction of choice: perhaps on the well-worn grounds that what a man chooses is predictable and will depend on various empirical factors (his heredity, psychological case history, education, etc.) outside his control. But this would be to mistake the point of reward and punishment,

1. See pp. 93–106.

at least as conceived from an egalitarian or liberal view-point. A reward or punishment is just or fair, on this view, not because it implies some judgement on a mysterious 'inner self' which is totally disconnected from the casual factors of the empirical world, but simply because it compensates for a misguided or selfish choice. What we have gained from our distinction shows us this: we could reasonably say that it was unfair to reward someone for the strength of a capacity (conscientiousness), when he did not *choose* to have a capacity of that strength: but we could not reasonably say that it was unfair to reward someone for the direction of a particular choice—precisely because in this instance we are rewarding him for what he *chooses*, not for what he *is*, even though what he chooses may be casually dependent on what he is. We have separated off those cases when a man is choosing freely—we assume that he has full knowledge of the facts, is not under threats or duress, and so forth—from the cases when a man is simply availing himself of powers which he may possess to a greater or lesser degree.

If our ultimate moral judgement is reserved for man's choice, intentions, and decisions, then it is, so to speak, for the *result of his deliberations* that we blame him, not for the actions which he does: for these may be governed by powers beyond his control (including his own strength or weakness of will). We may certainly blame him for not bringing some power more under his control, but only if his choice or intention would actually have done so: we are still blaming him for misguided deliberation, for not *setting himself* in the right direction. How far he can actually move in that direction is another matter.

c) *Equality and Competition*

How far does this help the egalitarian in setting up games or systems which are, in the fullest sense, fair? It is easy to conceive of a game in which choices or intentions are immediately translated into actions, so that the winner would be the player who made the best choices. This is the effect true of chess (assuming the players are not paralysed): or one could envisage a game of tennis in which (given sufficient technological devices) the ball would always go where the striker intended it to go. (We should have to count some choices as illegitimate, in order to prevent the receiver from choosing to be instantaneously transported to wherever the ball landed). But now the result depends on intelligence, or whatever special intellectual capability is needed for the game: and we are back to rewarding natural characteristics which are not equally shared by all men. We are rewarding choices, or the results of deliberation, but we are rewarding them for being intelligent choices, the results of skilled deliberation: and this is no more fair than any other game.

What the egalitarian wants to reward, of course, is *moral* choice. Suppose we have a social system in which we can verify a person's intentions, and agree upon their moral worth. We take into account, or arrange handicaps for, the varying abilities of people to carry out their intentions, but we reward the intentions alone. We assume that it does not require a special skill to have morally good intentions: that there are at least some occasions when anyone, with knowledge of the facts, can either set himself to do good or set himself to do evil. We then compensate for (reward) the good intentions, and also compensate for (punish) the bad ones. What are the objections to this?

There are three, all of which seem serious or fatal. First, although we might agree that there is not a 'special skill' for forming morally good intentions, yet plainly a man's intentions may depend ultimately on some causal factors outside his control (his heredity, psychic make-up, etc.): so that in effect we may find ourselves rewarding those with 'good' genes or a fortunate psychological case-history. The egalitarian may still say, as we have seen, that we are not rewarding them for their genes or case-history, but for the choices and intentions they actually make. But now this seems no more fair than rewarding people for making intelligent choices, which might depend on innate intellectual ability. The egalitarian may say that if we cannot fairly reward people for moral choices, then we cannot fairly reward them for anything: that the whole concept of fairness or justice dissolves at this point. This may be true: but he has still given no reason why rewards should be given for this particular thing, namely moral choice, rather than for some other. He has in effect admitted that the notion of fairness is wholly relative to a pre-existing set of rules. It may be the case that, on reflection, human beings cling most tenaciously to those particular rules that are framed so as to reward moral choice: but it has to be shown that they are right in doing so. We cannot show this from within the notions of justice and fairness, so to speak: we have to step outside them and find reasons of a different kind.

Secondly, such a system would not be a competitive system or a game. We were able to think of cases, like chess and the new version of tennis described above, in which choices and intentions alone were rewarded: but these were competitive games only because special skills were involved. The players had to *work out* what was 'the right thing to do' by virtue of their intelligence and tactical skill: they did not simply *choose* to do *the right thing* in a moral sense, whereby a person can already know the right thing, and then choose to do it. No competition is possible by the mere exercise of moral choice: competition demands a skill which the players deploy more or less effectively against each other. Even if you could have a system in which moral choices alone were rewarded, it would not be a competitive system: unless we attribute a special skill to making moral choices, in which case we have, as before, to justify rewarding this particular skill as against others.

Thirdly, such a system would in practice go against the egalitarian idea of justice as compensation. There is, no doubt, a sense in which the man who merely intends to do something wrong, without being able to take any steps to do it, gets away with something: and in which the man who sets himself to do some virtuous act, without actually doing it, loses something. We might say that the wicked man allows his selfish desires freer play, whereas the virtuous man's inhibitions of his desires costs him something: and we could, I suppose, compensate for these rather ethereal gains and losses. But we should normally suppose that any justice that should be applied to such cases ought to take the form of prickings or approbations of the individual conscience, perhaps backed by individual praise, blame, exhortation, or condemnation, rather than the form of some political or social rule. It would be a case for the individual or the individual's personal associates—priest, or friends, or counsellors—rather than the state and the law. For mere intention, at least in its direct consequences, affects no one but the individual who intends. The state is only interested in *attempted* murder—that is, in the taking of some actual steps in the direction of murder—not in the mere intention of murder. The intention must be present if punishment is justified: but it is only a necessary, not a sufficient, condition for political and social rules of justice. These rules compensate for something a person actually gets away with, or at least goes some way towards getting away with. The case is admittedly not a clear one: but we may roughly say that social rules, rules between people, are primarily concerned with the actual effects that one person has on others, like the rules of a game. We should not think it socially just to compensate a person for making *any* effort that costs him something, as when he climbs a mountain just to prove his own strength to himself: it has to be an effort which benefits society, as perhaps when he climbs Everest and brings prestige to his country.

It is interesting to observe what the egalitarian might now do when confronted with these objections. If he is still interested in constructing ideally fair games or systems, he might support only those in which there is no question of reward. To achieve this, we could adopt either one of two methods. First, we could carry out a programme of compensation or equalisation in a very real and literal sense, by *making* everyone equal. This rather futuristic programme would involve equalising all those features which are or might be used in competition, since any such competition would on this view be unfair: we should have to equalise physical strength, intelligence, beauty,[1] and so forth. The result would be a set of identical people, to all intents and purposes. Of course this would be undesirable for all sorts of reasons: what concerns us here is whether this fulfils the egalitarian's principles.

Unless his principle simply *is* that everyone ought to be the same, uniformity offers him no help. For he has only succeeded in producing a game or a social system of a very curious type. Two identical people playing tennis, or striving for political office, might indeed be competing: but

1. As in L. P. Hartley's novel *Facial Justice*.

insofar as the result depends on their talents rather than on chance, neither could ever win. The game of tennis would never get beyond 40—40, since as soon as one player gained an advantage the other would at once win the next point and make it deuce again; or perhaps, since neither was the least bit better than the other, the very first rally of the match would be interminable, or last until both players dropped from exhaustion—presumably at exactly the same time. The politicians would be so equally matched that either the votes would come out exactly equal for each, or else the electorate would be totally unable to choose between them and not vote at all.

In practice this would reduce the competition to one of pure chance—the results would depend on which player won the toss, or on whether one politician happened to smile at exactly the right moment. This is the second way open to the egalitarian. But this too produces odd results. Games of chance are not competitive in the same way that games of skill are. There is a weak sense in which, in roulette or bingo, the players compete for the common stakes made up from each individual's pocket : but they do not really play *against* each other. Even if I directly face you, and we cut a pack of cards on the understanding that the one with the highest-ranking card wins, we are hardly playing against each other. The only real sense in which there is competition lies not in anything the players do, but simply in the fact that some of them can win.

The fact that they can win, however, presents the egalitarians with another difficulty. His support in a game of this kind seems inconsistent with his desire to compensate for the deficiencies of those who are handicapped by fate, which was the prime element in his conception of justice. If it is unfair for people to be better off because they are by chance born into rich families, it can hardly be fair for people to be better off because they happen to back the right number of the right horse by chance. If it is unjust that a person should have the misfortune to be struck by lightning, it is also unjust that he should have the misfortune to be chosen by lot to be fed to the Minotaur. The very element of the game which makes it more than just a silly ritual—i.e. the fact that you can win money—also seems to be its most unjust feature.

This suggests two other quite different principles to which the egalitarian might turn. First, we do not in fact think the existence of the games of bingo and roulette unjust, because nobody is compelled to play them. All the players have *agreed* to play. They have *chosen* the rules by which this particular piece of their lives is to be governed. We return here to a point made earlier about equal scope: perhaps the apparent impossibility of constructing games where there is an absolute equality of opportunity is not as disturbing as it seems. For the egalitarian may admit this impossibility (whilst still claiming that some games are preferable to others), but claim that his real concern is that everyone should have an equal voice in *constructing* the games. He might admit that all social systems were bound to be unfair in an absolute sense, since any system will favour one set of talents or skills over another: but if everyone has the same power as everyone else in deciding what system to have, he might be satisfied.

Secondly, the odd results of making all people uniform or all social activities like a lottery suggest that the egalitarian may be wanting to *do away with competition altogether*. If we remove particular skills and talents by making people uniform and go on to abolish games of chance by removing the possibility of winning, we have thereby abolished competitive games as a whole. We can engage in ritual, or exhibitions, or co-operative projects, but we cannot play or compete against each other. Even if we retain the possibility of winning, but make all activities into activities of pure chance, we have still cut down competition to a vast extent. Questions of justice, fairness, compensation, and so on no longer arise in this context, because people would be working together rather than against each other.

This would not abolish the necessity for rules. The members of an orchestra are governed by rules, and even in a sense have a ruler (the conductor). But they co-operate rather than compete: indeed the rules are designed to ensure co-operation rather than competition. The egalitarian may be demanding that society should be more like an orchestra and less like a gladiatorial contest in the Roman arena, (a) because the members of the orchestra perform of their own choice, whereas gladiators do not, and (b) because the members of the orchestra combine, whereas gladiators kill each other. These two principles of equality are, in my view, among the most important that the concept will yield: and I shall discuss the ideas on which they are based at some length later on.

PART TWO

EQUALITY
AS A FACT

IN considering equality as a political principle, and particularly the relationships between man and nature, two things will have impressed us. First, we found that the notions of natural similarity and human nature were far more fluid and uncertain than we had supposed. Sense could be made of these notions, but their particular application seemed to depend on all sorts of practical points—upon the kind of language we used, the kind of interests we had, and even upon the degree to which our scientific techniques had advanced. Secondly, we found that other notions of a quite different type kept cropping up: the notions of human choice, deliberation, intention, and intelligence.

This suggests two possible lines which the egalitarian can take, if he wants to assert equality as a fact, each of which has prima facie advantages and disadvantages. The advantage of resting his case on natural similarities is that, given the world as it is, these similarities seem comparatively easy to prove or disprove. It should be obvious, either that all men are, or that they are not, equal in respect of needing food, being liable to pain, having two legs, and so on. The disadvantage is that the world might change, so that what were once natural similarities may cease to be: or, more subtly, that we might come to see the world differently from the way in which we now see it, so that where we once saw similarities we now see differences and vice versa. Conversely, the advantage of resting his case on notions like the powers of choice and ratiocination is that these powers seem more immune to practical changes in the world, more inalienable and intrinsic to the nature of all men. But the corresponding disadvantage is the difficulty of making sense of these notions in the context of equality: even if we knew exactly what we were talking about when we used words like 'choice', 'intention', etc., it would not at once be clear why this entitled us to assert that all men were equal.

We may conveniently call these two possible kinds of equality 'accidental' and 'intrinsic'. Both are important: but the egalitarian is likely to be driven to a defence of the latter when he meets really tough opposition. The importance of defending accidental equality is that we do, after all, see the world in much the same way, at least in certain respects: we have fairly constant criteria, and a reasonably static world, *and the egalitarian can make capital out of this by forcing us to accept the consequences of our world-view. But there are those who, if only on particular points, see the world very differently, and who might therefore remain quite unmoved by any picture of accidental equality that others might accept: and there are even those who would be prepared to change the world and thereby wipe out this picture. Hence the egalitarian seeks to paint a picture of intrinsic equality which nobody can reasonably deny or obliterate.*

I

Accidental Equality

Part of the sense which lies behind 'All men are equal' can best be clarified by seeing how the egalitarian responds to a standard objection to his thesis. In defining 'equal' the dictionary used phrases like 'identical', 'on the same level', 'having the same . . .' etc. 'Equal' has thus a minimal meaning of 'the same' or 'similar'. But though 'equal' implies *some* kind of similarity assertions about equality are only comprehensible where the context is given or understood: that is, where we know *in what respect* the two things or people are thought to be similar. Now if we interpret the egalitarian's assertion 'All men are equal' as 'All men are equally ———', we can ask him to fill in the blank. Moreover, it seems that he must fill in the blank with some adjective of degree: for he is apparently making a comparison to the effect that all men possess some quality or qualities to the same degree or the same extent—that every man is *just as* tall, saintly, intelligent, etc., *as* his neighbour. Now his difficulty is that, when we measure the degree to which various people possess an empirical characteristic, this degree evidently varies. How can the egalitarian defend himself against this? There are two ways in which he might do so.

(a) The first way consists of accepting the above statement of his difficulty but denying that the degree to which people possess certain characteristics always varies. He could claim that we should not press our criteria of similarity too far. It is true that there is no particular human characteristic which is identical in the case of all men, if we mean by this that we can always detect some difference if we try hard enough. But this is true of all similarities, not only human ones. A pair of scales may be equally balanced: yet we can still say that the weights on either side are not 'really' equal or not 'really' the same, if we mean that a more finely balanced pair of scales might show a difference. Two lines can be of equal lengths: yet if we insist on measuring them in micromilli-metres we could prove one to be a little longer. Identical twins, we might say, are not 'really' identical: some test might always detect a minute variation. But this leads to the paradoxical view that nothing is really ever the same as anything else. The paradox is resolved when we see that we use words like 'the same', 'similar', 'equal', and 'identical' when we are making comparisons, and that we set up the terms of the comparison to suit ourselves. Sometimes we use a crude standard of measurement, and sometimes a finer one: and sometimes we might use a different standard altogether in order to measure something different.

To put it another way, whether or not we attribute equality to things depends on the context we are in: and this context can vary in two significant ways. First, the context may change because we want to apply different criteria altogether. To say 'All the houses in this street are equal', once we have got over the apparent unintelligibility of saying this without giving a particular context, implies that there are some criteria or some standards of measurement in reference to which the assertion is true. Thus the houses might be equally rated, or equally beautiful, or equally capacious. Whether we assert or deny that all the houses are equal depends on whether we are judging from the viewpoint of a rating officer, an artist, or a mother of six. Secondly, it may vary in regard to the fineness of measurement required. Suppose we are grading the respective intelligence of men and pigs. Now it might be the case that some men were as stupid as most pigs, and some pigs as clever as most men. If that were so, we would not say either that all men were equally intelligent, or that all pigs were. But if, as is no doubt the case, all men fall roughly into the same I.Q. group, then we could quite reasonably report this by the assertions 'All men are equally intelligent' and 'all pigs are equally intelligent'. We should be denying the first possibility, i.e. that some men or some pigs were wildly unlike others in point of I.Q. In the same way we might consider it roughly true that all girls who modelled clothes were equally slim, but false that all secretaries and all young mothers were. But if we changed our context, and conducted measurements solely *within* a particular class, we should not talk like this. Within the class 'man' and 'pig', all men and all pigs are not equally intelligent: and within the class 'model', not all models are equally slim.

(b) The second way consists of denying that he has to fill in the blank with an adjective of degree. The egalitarian might say that all he wishes to assert is that there are certain similarities amongst men, not that there are certain qualities which they all possess to the same degree. Thus some people are much more sensitive to pain than others. But the egalitarian may mean merely that men are all, equally,—the commas are important—liable to pain: i.e. one man is liable to pain *just as* another is, not *just as much as* another is.

This is certainly a very different sense of 'equally'; and some people might regard it as rather contemptible, though it is certainly found in good English. But 'equally' has many uses which are looser than this: sometimes it just means 'also' or 'as well', like the French '*également*' or the Latin '*aeque*'. In any case, it seems that we must allow this defence on the part of the egalitarian, even if it means rejecting the translations of 'All men are equal' into 'All men are equally ——', and translate instead into 'All men are equal in *that* they are ——', filling in the blank not with an adjective of degree but with some other adjective, such as 'two-legged' or 'mortal', which does not admit of degrees.

What the egalitarian is now asserting is simply that men are similar or the same in a certain respect: and this seems legitimate, in that 'equal' (if not 'equally') can bear this rather wide sense, and does not have to be tied down to measurement of degree. Alternatively, he may use a word or phrase that *can* function as an adjective of degree, such as 'liable to pain' or 'needing food': but the kind of equality he is now asserting will as before not be an equality of degree, but merely a similarity. To use another example, an egalitarian might say 'All men are equally in need of food'. This is ambiguous between 'One man needs food as much as another', i.e. all men alike need food, which is true: and 'One man needs as much food as another', i.e. all men need the same amount of food, which is false (large people need more food than small people). He is not using 'food-needing' as an adjective of degree, but merely as delimiting a class into which all men fall.

These are in fact the only two possible interpretations of 'equal' in this particular context. If we say 'All so-and-sos are equal' or 'All so-and-sos are equally such-and-such', we could only mean *either* that all so-and-sos, as a class, share some characteristic in the same degree and the same extent as compared with other classes of things (the first defence): *or* that all so-and-sos have certain common characteristics, though not necessarily in the same degree (the second defence). It might be thought that a third interpretation was possible (though it would make 'All men are equal' certainly false): i.e. a measurement *within* the class of so-and-sos, *and* a similarity of degree. Thus we say 'These two lines are equal', measuring within the class of lines, and also saying that the lines are just as long as each other, not merely that they both have length. But the introduction of 'all' in 'All so-and-sos are equal' obviates this possibility. For the only purpose of measuring degree *within* a class is to separate and distinguish some members of the class from others: there would be no point in making comparisons at all, if all members of the class were the same. This is why 'These two lines are equal' is sensible in a way in which 'All lines are equal' is silly: and the same applies to every statement of the form 'All so-and-sos are equal', if interpreted in this third way. We could certainly say things like 'All the lines on this blackboard are equal', or 'All the boys in this class are of equal intelligence', but the additional phrases serve to distinguish the lines of this blackboard from other lines and the boys in this class from other boys: we do not really mean *all* lines or *all boys whatsoever*. Hence we need not feel cheated by the impossibility of applying this third interpretation to 'All men are equal', for the impossibility is a logical one. It is not, as we might at first have thought, that the egalitarian makes such a claim, and that the claim turns out to be false: it is rather that neither he nor anyone else can intelligibly make or dispute such a claim at all.

Given the latitude gained by these two defences, we can see that the egalitarian has more to say than might be supposed.

First, using the defence which allows a strong sense of
'equally', there are a great many characteristics and capacities
in respect of which men are equal *in comparison with other
entities*, though not in comparison with each other. It is a
contingent fact, which might well be otherwise, that these
characteristics and capacities can always be predicated, to an
approximately equal degree, of all those entities that we call
men. We could quite easily conceive a situation in which
some men felt no more pain than stones feel, or were
no more capable of loving their homes than ants are capable
of loving their ant-hills. Indeed, the weakness of the egalitarian's case here is not that it is unfalsifiable or hopelessly
vague, but rather that it may be factually false; perhaps
there *are* men who feel no more pain than stones or who can
love no better than ants. But even if he has to modify his
assertion to 'All—or nearly all—men are equal', he plainly
has a great deal to say that is true. What we may call the
common humanity of men, their common destiny, and their
common condition, is a hard fact.

Secondly, using the looser sense of 'equally,' the egalitarian
can legitimately expand the notion of common humanity
still further. In this sense he does not even have to show that
men share certain common characteristics to a degree which
is not found in other entities : he has only to show that they
are similar to each other in certain ways. Thus, we can say
that men are equal in that they can all use a language and
feel pain : we do not have to assert that they are all equally
skilled in using a language or equally sensitive to pain. Again,
men are equally liable to misfortune and death : but we do
not say that all meet the same misfortunes or that they all die
at the same age.

It would be wrong to think that the assertion of his common humanity and destiny amounted to a tautology or plati-
tude of which we needed to be reminded, like the words
whispered into the victor's ear during a Roman triumph—
'Remember thou art mortal'. 'All men are equal' does not
mean 'All men are men', nor even 'All men are the same in
their humanity', if we take 'in their humanity' to contain
no more than is meant or implied in the phrase 'being a man'.
In other words, there are points of similarity about men
which are not implied in the *definition* of 'man' or 'human

being'. Thus we do not *mean* by the word 'man' any of the things which psychologists or other scientists tell us are common to all men, such as 'having an unconscious mind', or 'possessing such-and-such a capacity for the storage of memories'. We could not mean this, because most of us do not even know about such things. We do not even include 'mortal' in our definition, though we know that death comes to all: 'an immortal man' is not a contradiction.

The definition of man is not in question here, and if it were the question would be very open: and rightly, because we have no standards of comparison. We can imagine cases of entities that were otherwise man-like but did not have a human shape, or human intelligence, or human desires, and we can ask ourselves which of these characteristics is essential to the concept of man: but we might very well be uncertain about the answer, which would in any case be a matter for our own decision. From this we can see both the strength and weakness of the claim that all men are equal, interpreting this as the claim that all men have a common humanity and a common destiny. Provided we base it firmly on empirical similarities amongst men, the *truth* of the claim is not in serious doubt. These similarities plainly exist. But the *relevance* of the claim depends on how important these similarities are: and importance is a matter of value rather than a matter of fact. Similarities and differences such as colour, facial features, shape of skull and so on, are not stressed by the egalitarian, because these are not thought to be relevant to the way men ought to be *treated*. The egalitarian is concerned with men's wants, needs, abilities, happiness, achievements, and satisfaction: it is their similarities in these respects, or in respects which bear on these, that he wants to stress. But these similarities are only relevant to the way men ought to be treated if we *count* them as relevant. If we think, as perhaps most of us do, that our behaviour towards other people should be influenced by some consideration of their wants, needs, abilities, etc., then it is helpful to be told that these are common to all men: helpful, if only because it enables us to make generalisations about our behaviour towards other men based on the similarities that all men share. But if we think quite other things to be important, such as their colour, facial features, or shape of skull, and these things are not common to all men, then we shall not be influenced by similarities in their wants and needs.

The egalitarian assumes that our criteria of importance are related to human happiness and the satisfaction of human desires. Of course these particular criteria have not been shown to be logically necessary: it is quite possible for somebody to prefer criteria which at least appear to be different, such as self-denial and self-sacrifice, or the will of God, or what their consciences tell them, or what the Communist Party says. But if we allow the egalitarian his assumption—it is one which I shall try to prove later—then a study of the empirical facts might make him a present of these two points:

1 Those features of the human mind and the human condition which are common to all men may be the most important for human happiness, because the features which classes of creatures have in common tend to be those which are the most basic to their natures, and hence most influential. Things like the need for food, sex, health, friendship, and love, the avoidance of pain, the fear and the inevitability of death, in a word our earliest and most basic biological and psychological features, may seem more relevant to happiness than our more specific differences in tastes, abilities, and needs. A man's capacity to do philosophy is less important than his capacity to love: his death, which he shares with all other men, is of greater ultimate significance to him than his social status, which he does not: and his avoidance of pain and disease may count for more than his avoidance of stupidity, bad taste, or even an unsuccessful career.

2 Similarities, it has often been said, unite human beings, whereas differences divide them. In so far as our happiness depends on unity rather than division, there is thus a very strong practical argument for stressing similarities. The importance of unity may be presented in an infinite number of contexts, varying from the obvious menace of a disunited world which may blow itself up at any minute, to the relevance of mutual need and communication for happiness in the context of personal relationships.

The bare possibility of establishing such points ought to

show that the egalitarian is not necessarily behaving arbitrarily in insisting on the overwhelming importance of certain similarities, even though these be accidental rather than intrinsic. But it also, of course, shows that the whole of this part of his case badly needs the backing of a much more solid picture, or ideal, of human happiness and morality. I hope to build up such a picture as we proceed.

2

Intrinsic Equality

Let us return for a moment to the egalitarian's difficulty in giving a translation of 'All men are equal'. In the last section we represented him as accepting a rendering in terms of 'All men are equally ———' and by virtue of a good deal of hard argument, in which the sense of 'equally' was pressed to its limits, he was able to give a fair amount of sense and importance to the original proposition. But the whole trend of his arguments does not strike one as altogether plausible or convincing. Not that the arguments were false: rather that they seemed to have been scraped up from the bottom of the barrel, and to misrepresent the general intention of 'All men are equal'. Few egalitarians would, I think, feel satisfied with the amount of weight we have so far attached to the assertion.

Suppose now he offers quite a different translation—'All men are *equals*'. This interpretation may appear, at first glance, as a deliberate and wilful attempt to blur the distinctions between natural equality and equality of status that we were at such pains to make.[1] For if 'All men are equals' is taken to mean that all men have an equal status, it seems plainly false: for the rules and ordinances of society do not grant all men an equal status—indeed, it is just this that egalitarians complain of. If the egalitarian now says something like 'Ah, but all men have a *natural* equality of status', adding that this natural equality ought to be mirrored in our artificially made rules and ordinances, he seems not to have understood the distinction: for, according to the account we gave, equality of status is, essentially, not

1. See pp. 40 and following.

a natural thing but a man-made one. On the other hand, if 'All men are equals' is taken to mean that they are similar in a certain natural quality or attribute—as a man might say 'I'm his equal in strength'—then he has not offered a new translation at all, but must be content with the translation 'All men are equally ——'. This argument is, in my view, too slick: and I shall try to maintain that there is a sense in which men have a natural equality of status.

a) Common Indispensability

One way in which we might be inclined to react against the view that some people 'just are inferior' is by claiming a kind of similarity among men which arises from their existence in society and the social roles that they play. This is the similarity to which we point when we say things like 'Privates are just as necessary as generals for winning wars', or 'Dustmen are just as important as dukes'.

The point here is not that the roles are similar *as roles*. Plainly this is the reverse of the truth: in terms of military status, a general is the superior of a private, and in terms of social status, dukes are 'more important' than privates and dustmen. But we are here referring to the artificial equality or inequality of status. The point is rather that there is one highly significant similarity between all social roles: namely, that they all have a part to play, particularly if a society has some kind of common purpose. The privates in an army are just as important as the generals for the purposes of winning wars; we could not do without them. In the same way we need to keep the streets clean just as much as we need people in the House of Lords; so that dustmen are just as important as dukes. Both are indispensable.

Whatever kinds of social ranking or social structure we may devise, the indispensability of the individual components remains. If, for example, we have a capitalist society in which the roles of the advertiser and salesman are part of the social game, they are *ipso facto* a *necessary* part. Of course, we can change the game and ban advertising, thereby probably altering our economy radically: just as we could devise some new card-game played without the lower denominations of cards. But as long as the social rule exists, it is necessary to the game because we cannot play that particular game without it.

Suppose, however, that we can do without privates and dustmen and advertisers, because we have machines which will do all the work we need: suppose also that we decide to do without women, if we can invent servo-mechanisms and incubators to replace them. The egalitarian would still object to treating these people as inferiors rather than equals. There are various possible grounds for objection: and we would, perhaps, most naturally think of framing our objections in terms of human rights, or in terms of the rights of the individual as against the state. Jews and morons, slaves and women, we would say, are *people*, and we owe them respect as people whether or not they contribute to the purposes of society. But we could put this point differently: so differently that it amounts to a different point, more closely connected with our original idea about individuals as contributors: that they all possess characteristics which could, in principle, take the form of essential social roles. The egalitarian would hold that our choice of the aims and purposes of society must be governed by this fact: that is, by the natural equality of all men as potential contributors. ✓

This is not, as it may at first sight seem, just a rather long-winded way of saying that we ought not to exclude certain groups from society. What the egalitarian accuses his opponent of, in this context, is not the immorality of killing off Jews or the senile, on the grounds that they have a right to live: the accusation is that if we do this, we are in some sense *cheating*. To frame a human society in the fullest sense is to frame a society for all human beings: we cannot pick and choose our materials. Human beings are the data on which we have to work: to reject any of them, on this view, is always to some degree a confession of failure.

The point here may be seen by considering an extreme case. Suppose I wield absolute power, and consider myself the acme of human perfection. In order to produce as perfect a world as possible, I kill everyone else and sit alone in my glory. The human race, now consisting of myself alone, may now have a very high intelligence, be racially pure, possess complete freedom, and enjoy all these things which we might think desirable. But it could not be said that I had succeeded in framing a human *society*. Now suppose I kill everyone except for a very few close friends. I can now claim to have a society, since I am no longer alone: but there will be two objections to what I have done. First it might be claimed that my society is likely to be rather dull and lacking in variety, since I have excluded so many different talents and contributions from it: and second, it is only in a rather trivial sense that I have framed a *human* society. What I have done is to frame a society of my closest friends, much as the Nazi extremists wanted to frame not a human society, but an Aryan one.

To take a parallel, suppose I have at my disposal a large number of bricks, slabs, beams, and so on. If I simply place what I take to be the most perfect brick on the building site I have not even made a building. Now if I put two bricks on their ends and another over the top I can perhaps be said to have built something; but, first, what I have built is not very exciting: and, secondly, I have not addressed myself very seriously to the task of building as such. I shall not need to study architecture, since the study of architecture is supposed to help in solving problems that only arise if we are trying to build something complex. I do not have any problems to solve, because I have simply disregarded the bulk of my materials.

In the same way the person who is prepared to exclude certain groups from society does not need political theory: for the problems of political theory arise from trying to balance the existing claims and characteristics of existing human beings, and weld them into some kind of harmony. To exclude large numbers of human beings is to cheat, to abandon the notion of political theory and the task of framing a society for human beings. Thus if I were faced with a large class of children, I could no doubt produce peace and quiet, and a state of perfect discipline, in the classroom by making one child read the Bible and giving all the others a half-holiday: but I could not claim to be educating them.

These considerations do not have the force of strict argument: they represent a particular view of life which is not logically compulsory. It is logically open to anybody, for all that we have said so far, to deny the value of bringing as many people as possible into society, and to deny that the aims and purposes of society should be based on the contributions of existing individuals rather than vice versa. The kind of equality which we are now considering seems ultimately to throw us back on certain very general views about human beings—views which are too general to be described simply as 'moral'. If we entertain these views, the considerations here advanced will help to give them shape and point: but we need still to clarify the views themselves and to defend them.

b) Common Freedom and Common Choice

I do not think that the points made so far, important as they are, lie at the heart of egalitarianism as expressed in such assertions as 'All men are equal'. They are, perhaps, the sort of points which might most readily spring to mind and be most easily expressed: and for that reason it is possible that, in particular historical contexts, it was these points which men were most concerned to make. Thus, if we are anxious to change a law whereby people of one race can be tortured and those of another race cannot be, we shall be likely to point out simply that both races are equally liable to pain. Again, in the case of dukes and dustmen, we need only to say that both jobs are equally essential. But as we have seen, there are plenty of difficult cases in which these points seem insufficient; and it is for this reason that many philosophers have tried to show the existence of a human equality which covers all cases.

That this is not merely an academic exercise on the part of philosophers, but an attempt to clarify what really lies at the back of our minds when we talk of fundamental human equality, can be seen if we consider more closely the case of a creature who could not be said to share in our common humanity or social indispensability, but whom nevertheless we might regard as an equal. Martians, whose bodies, feelings, wants, abilities and so on were utterly unlike our own, might in specific respects be our superiors (if they were much cleverer than we, for instance), or our inferiors (if they were much more stupid, or lazier). But whether we regarded them as essentially on an equality with ourselves would depend on whether they were *rational beings*; whether, like us, they had the power to form intentions, make decisions, choose freely, and pursue their ends intelligently.

If they did not have these powers, we should regard them as dissimilar to ourselves in a respect far more important than any other. They might be physically stronger than we are, as are elephants, or able to calculate more rapidly and efficiently, as computing machines can do: but we should not consider that they had equal rights, or that they ought to be given an equal voice in whatever transactions took place between Earth and Mars, or that their purposes should weigh as heavily as our own. Indeed, we *could* not treat them as equals in these ways even if we desired. For the notions of exercising a right, having an equal voice, and entertaining purposes only apply to creatures who are, like ourselves, rational: for only such creatures could comprehend them. If the Martians were not rational beings, they would necessarily be excluded from those many activities which are only open to rational beings.

It is important to observe that our inability to treat them as equals in this way would not imply anything to the effect that we were entitled to treat them with less *respect* or *consideration*. Nor would we necessarily wish to do so. There are many people who treat their infant offspring, and even their animals, with far more respect and consideration than they give to their equals. We might even think that some inanimate object, as for instance a great work of art, was in a sense more *valuable* than a human being who was our equal. But there would be a certain kind of respect which we could not give the Martians—the respect due to those who are rational like ourselves.

A clear example of this distinction is afforded in some personal relationships. A man may have a wife who is very like himself in many ways: he may esteem her highly, minister assiduously to her wants and needs, subordinate his own desires to hers, and value her more highly than he values himself; yet he might still not regard her as an equal. In his eyes she might be no more than a very valuable pet. Conversely, another man might fail to do all these things, and yet treat his wife as an equal. The crux here is whether the wife is treated as an equal *partner*, as somebody whose will *counts for as much as* her husband's, as somebody who is afforded equal *status* in the business of making decisions and carrying out plans and purposes.

It is an observable and demonstrable fact that certain entities in the world possess powers to which we refer when we use words like 'will', 'choice', 'intention', 'intelligence', and many others. These powers are no doubt causally connected with certain physiological facts, and because of our ignorance of many of these facts they seem mysterious. This gives us no reason to place the powers in another 'supernatural' or 'transcendent' world, though in speaking of them we have to use language quite different from the language we use in speaking of entities that lack these powers. Just as in the history of evolution the inorganic merges almost imperceptibly into the organic, and non-life gradually produced what we call life, so the non-rational and non-intelligent may by slow degrees have thrown up certain entities that are rational and intelligent. There is a difference in kind, that has to be marked in language, between the rational and the non-rational, as between life and non-life. But there is no sort of *magic* about it. There is no logical reason why we should not be able to produce a rational creature by artificial methods, just as we now create children by the natural processes of procreation.

What is uniquely important about these powers is that they enable every person who shares them—we might simply say, every *person*—to create his own values and his own rules. Meaningful disagreements can only arise within the framework of created human agreement: in particular, agreement about language and about the criteria of value. In order to dispute significantly, we depend on accepted rules of one kind or another: if we did not, we could fight or impede each other, as animals do, but we could not disagree. There are some rules, to which we usually refer as 'laws of thought', which it would be very hard to conceive as anything but essential for any rational creature: perhaps the most basic of these is the law of non-contradiction. Other rules seem basically due to the fact that human beings share a common biological inheritance and common sense experience, so that it is natural for us to agree on a common language to denote these experiences. Other rules again, of a logically different kind, denote fairly widespread agreement about values, and seem to depend upon desires and dislikes which are widely shared amongst human beings.

Think again of a Martian, rational as ourselves, but with a totally different body, sense-organs, and desires. Let us indulge in science fiction, and imagine him to consist of waves and electrons: able to perceive what he would call 'colours' on the infra-red level and below: without what we call a sense of hearing: desiring things that to us seemed almost incomprehensible, such as a certain type of radio-wave, or to be bathed in cosmic rays. Such a creature would, as we might say, live in a different world from ourselves. We could not say that his world was 'less real' than ours, or that the 'colours' he perceives are 'not really' colours: or at least we could say this, but we should simply be reiterating our own ideas of what is real, or what really is a colour, in a language based on those ideas. Anything below the infra-red level, or above the ultra-violet, is not a colour, because it would not be what we meant by the word 'colour': but we have framed this criterion for the application of the word because it happens to suit our own particular sense-perceptions. The Martian's world is as real as our own: and this is simply to say that he suffers from no more delusions or hallucinations than we do, that he has built up a world out of his experience just as we have.

It seems equally plain that we cannot disagree with the Martian's criteria of value either, and for just the same reason: we have no common ground. If we care to stand on his ground and accept his ultimate ends—to experience radio-waves and cosmic rays—then we may be able to argue with him about what he actually does and thinks. We can point out certain facts to him, or criticise flaws in his reasoning, where these facts and flaws bear on his achievement of these ends. We might even think that his criteria were curiously disconnected from his actual nature—it might be that radio-waves tended to make him ill, and cosmic rays were liable to kill him. But it might be characteristic of Martians that they like being ill and running the risk of being killed. In any case, it would be his choice, and if we want to say that he had chosen wrongly, we should find ourselves at a loss for any criteria of value that would be common between him and ourselves.

This somewhat fantastic example brings home a truth which we are apt to forget when dealing with fellow-humans, though it applies equally to them: namely that if two people differ in their ultimate criteria of value or rules for behaviour, then—precisely because these criteria and rules are ultimate—they have no higher criteria or rules by which to settle their difference. This is a point which both analytic and existentialist philosophers have hammered home in the last few decades. It does not follow that we have to abandon any idea that ethics can be rational, but it does follow that our criteria of value are in the last analysis based upon human choice: and this has consequences for the notion of equality which are of the greatest importance.

The point can be made roughly by saying that all human beings have the same *status* as choosers and creators of value. When we disagree with somebody about ultimate criteria, it becomes important to notice what language we can intelligibly use. We can certainly disapprove of, or condemn, or show hostility towards his ultimate values: we can say words to the effect of 'I'm against them' or 'I choose quite differently', or 'I shall fight that tooth and nail'. But it is only in this sense intelligible to say that his values are not *good* or not the *right values*. For both 'good' and 'right' are normally used, not simply as terms of purely personal preference, but in reference to certain criteria in virtue of which we count things as good or right. We can question our criteria of goodness up to a certain point, by referring them to higher criteria: but the time comes when we run out of ammunition. The point here is not substantially different from the impossibility of talking about 'the right time' unless we already have agreed rules about what counts as the right time. If it is five o'clock in the U.S.A. and ten o'clock in England, what is 'the right time'? The question is unintelligible.

It seems unintelligible to say, therefore, that one person is a better valuer or a better chooser of values than another, if we press the matter to its limits. If two clocks run consistently but at different speeds the only justification we have for saying that one is better as a time-keeper than the other lies in a common agreement to refer the issue to Greenwich Observatory, or the sun, or some other accepted standard

D

of measurement. It is sense to say that one tape-measure measures more accurately than the other, because we can compare them with the metre bar in Paris, but to ask whether the metre bar is a good measurer of metres is not sense—the metre bar *defines* the metre.

Because each man can shape his own ends and can choose his own values (despite the fact that many men accept values rather than choose them), there comes a point at which it is impossible to say that one man is superior or inferior to another: for 'superior' and 'inferior' only make sense in terms of some rule or criterion which is itself man-made. We cannot find any exact parallel here, for all other cases of human judgement or activity fall short of this point: but their inadequacies may perhaps help to make the point .

One sovereign law-making body, for instance, cannot be said to behave in a more legal or law-abiding way than another when it makes laws: for such a body does not follow the law, but defines it. One umpire or referee is less observant or well informed than another, thereby referring the issue to higher criteria. But the decisions of all umpires and referees are equally 'final'. Since they create their own values, men are rather more like bidders in an auction, who do not guess or judge the value of the objects, but make that value by their bids. In this vital respect, then, men are —to quote the dictionary definition of 'equal' again—'neither less nor greater' but 'on the same level': and it seems quite unexceptionable to describe them as equals in this respect. This is a natural and not an artificial equality: the whole point, indeed, is that it does not depend on any status which we give to particular people as creators of value, but upon the natural abilities of rational beings. The practical moral implication of this, which we shall draw more fully in subsequent parts, are not hard to see. For if one's morality pays any attention at all to the facts of human nature, to the actual powers and capacities of men, and also to the principle that similar cases demand similar treatment, then this particular similarity amongst men is plainly one of the most important. It will be the most reasonable basis for the belief that men have the equal right to decide their own destinies, since they have an equal capacity to do so: and for the belief they have an equal right to make their wills and purposes felt—to actualise them in the world—since the will and purposes of each man are ultimately as valid as those of his neighbour.

Moreover this kind of equality can be pressed much further than other forms of natural equality. There is a rough similarity between men in many respects: they are all in some degree intelligent, liable to pain, and so on. But they do not have these characteristics to the same degree: we have to be content with general similarities. This also applies to certain empirical characteristics which have a moral aspect, such as those qualities to which we refer by such names as 'will-power', 'purposiveness', and 'determination'. These are in some loose sense measurable: one man possesses more of them than another. But the ability to form intentions and to value, to choose, and to have purposes, although it is empirically observable, is not in the same way quantitive. There is no difficulty about saying that one man is more purposive, or determined, or responsible than another; but it would be odd to say that one man is more able to form intentions or make choices than another.

It is not nonsense to say this, however. We could imagine ourselves saying of a man who, for instance, spent most of his time asleep or in intense pain that he was less able to make choices and decisions: though we should probably say that he had less *chance* of doing so. We could say of a madman, or even of somebody highly neurotic, perhaps, that he was less able: certainly we would use phrases like 'he can never make up his mind', 'he doesn't really value anything', 'he just drifts', 'he never seriously intends to do anything', 'he doesn't really choose, he just finds himself doing things', and so on. But these are extreme cases: and we should feel inclined to say that, to the extent that a person's powers of choice and decision were diminished, he was less of a *person*. Madmen are people only by courtesy: and prolonged pain can reduce people to the level of animals. In so far as human beings remain human, therefore, they possess these powers to an equal degree.

This is not just a logical sleight-of-hand, an attempt to prove this absolute equality by a pre-emptive definition of what it is to be human. For it is not a mere accident that we should continue to count as human such people as possessed

other human characteristics (such as the capacity to love or feel pain) in a very slight degree, or not at all. We could call such people 'inhuman', but we would not mean it literally. In considering when to count children as people, or whether to count robots, animals, morons, Martians, and madmen as people, it is this central characteristic, the ability to choose and decide, that we always have in mind. We are concerned with whether the entity, as we say, 'has a will of its own'; and this is not a quantitative matter, though there may be borderline cases. Either it has a will of its own, or it has not.

If somebody chooses to do something which we think to be very silly or wicked, such as becoming an opium addict or a mass murderer, we are often tempted to deny that his powers of choice and deliberation are equal to our own. This denial may take the unsophisticated form of assuming that since our own values are so obviously correct, there must be something wrong with the person who overlooks or transgresses them: this is simply to miss the point made earlier, that intrinsic equality *lies behind* each man's values. But we might make a more subtle objection: the objection that, since each man's choices are necessarily limited by the language he uses and the facts available to him, some people are more able to choose, or able to choose more widely or more freely, than others. Thus if I am a member of a primitive tribe that follows a very narrow pattern of moral behaviour and has no contact with the outside world, I shall have neither the language nor the knowledge to make choices which fall far outside this pattern: and my imagination is also likely to be restricted by the limitations imposed by my environment.

This objection fails, however, because it assumes that a wide range of choices is to be preferred to a narrow one. Most of us would probably accept such an assumption: but it is not logically necessary, and it is quite possible to hold that human beings ought to consider only a narrow range of choices. The primitive tribe might easily claim that their moral choices and behaviour were the best possible, and that it was a waste of time—or positively dangerous—to look further afield. We could only persuade them otherwise by referring them to some criterion that they already had— perhaps the desire to make progress, improve their society, increase their power, or whatever—and show that they needed a wider range of choices in order to satisfy that criterion: but then we should be treating them as equals, by arguing on their criteria rather than writing them off as 'inferior' or 'limited' and imposing our own criteria on them. Similarly, in considering those very silly or very wicked people whom we feel inclined to dismiss as 'mad', 'not in their right mind', or 'in no position to choose for themselves', we must carefully distinguish between strongly disagreeing with their choices on the one hand, and denying that they have the power of choice on the other.

Exactly what tests we should employ in deciding whether someone had the power of choice or not is a hard question. Certainly he would need to be able to use language, and to represent his intentions to himself, if not to others. It seems also as if he would have to possess, in however small a degree, the power to reflect and deliberate: otherwise (to put it roughly) he would not be really *choosing*, but just reacting. In psychological terms, we should try to establish that the man had some kind of ego, a part of himself which was not just a swirling battleground of conflicting fears and desires but was capable of some sort of deliberate control and decision. Those with severe mental illness might well make us hesitate before deciding one way or the other. I incline to think, however, that even a faint flicker of genuine choice would be sufficient to establish the existence of a person, possessed of intrinsic equality (and whatever rights we might accept as following from this). A person who was only sane on Monday, and behaved like an animal for the rest of the week, would still be a person: after all, we count ourselves as people even though for a third of our life we are incapable of choice because we are asleep.

We must also remember that, in the practical workings of society, choices are rarely presented to individual people with that degree of clarity which my examples may have suggested. For instance, by industrialising a primitive agricultural society we do far more than merely change the economy and the technology: we transform the whole way of life of that society, because the behaviour appropriate to a new means of production inevitably spills over into other forms of behaviour. Thus a capitalistic and technological culture may perhaps demand certain kinds of responsibility and certain virtues in the individual—thrift, punctuality, self-discipline, independence—and the importance of these virtues is likely to be reproduced in the morality and religion of that society. My point here is that this process is likely to be unrecognised by the individuals: they will find themselves unconsciously adopting new values, and taking new things for granted. But this is not to say that they do not have the power of choice, in the sense I have been trying to give to the phrase: it is rather to say that, due to limitations on their understanding and their unconscious acceptance of the forms of life with which this economic process has saddled them, they have not realised their power of choice in this particular area.

The notion of 'having a will of one's own' is also importantly ambiguous. There are plenty of cases where people suffer, either on occasions or permanently, from what we may call atrophy of the will: but it is not this sense of 'will' on which intrinsic equality is based. A man may lack willpower or determination, or may not be able to make an effort: but we cannot for that reason count him as an inferior, or claim that he does not choose or that his choices should not count. Certainly, he will have to do more than merely *imagine* some state of affairs to himself or merely *feel a desire* for something: he must *will* it, in the sense of setting himself to some course of action: he must specifically desire to actualise it. There may not be any actual steps which he can take (either because he lacks will-power or for some other reason): but the position must be such that he would take some steps if he could. Given such a position—and this is usually not hard to verify—we must allow him to have chosen.

It is worth reminding ourselves of the relevance of these points to the possible interpretations of 'All men are equal' which we might use in reference to intrinsic equality. If we use the first defence mentioned in the last section, whereby we are measuring the class of men against other classes of entities, then we can represent intrinsic equality as an equality of powers, abilities or capacities. In this sense we must admit that *within* the class of men, all men are *not* equally capable of choice, desire, will-power, determination, effort, rational reflection, and so forth. But they may be allowed a comparative equality, as measured against the powers of other creatures. On the other hand, if we use the second defence, whereby we refer simply to a common characteristic, we have to distinguish carefully between two possibilities. First, we can say that all men are, equally, capable of will-power, effort, and rational reflection (though not in the same degree): and, secondly, we can describe this equality without using adjectives of degree at all. Thus there is a sense to words and phrases like 'rational', 'conscious', 'having a will of one's own', 'choosing', 'purposive', and 'self-regulating' which does not permit one intelligibly to say that one person is more rational, conscious, etc., than another. Thus there is a sense in which one machine (a computer) may be more self-regulating than another (a simple thermostatic device): but there is also a sense in which a machine is either self-regulating or not. This is not to deny the possibility of borderline cases, about which we might feel doubtful and which we would have to settle by a decison. But amongst men such borderline cases are very rare.

All these interpretations can be accepted: but the real importance of intrinsic equality lies in the last; for as we have seen, the key point is that the equality which derives from the powers of choice, of creating one's own values, of having purposes, and of following rules has a significance quite unlike the significance of accidental similarities amongst men. For these former characteristics are the basis for language, and for the whole apparatus of judgement which depends on the criteria of language. Intrinsic equality rests on the fact that all human beings come into a particular category or mode of being. Their varying abilities to reflect and deliberate, to state their values or the rules they follow and to exercise will-power or effort, do not constitute the major issue. The point is rather that no human being can escape from his general category (except by suicide or by being reduced to an animal level), and above all that inclusion in this category gives all human beings a similar status vis-à-vis their fellows.

Moreover, no other conceivable power or ability can seem so important to us as the ability to choose and create value, because it is in terms of this ability that the im-

portance of other abilities is defined. We might imagine
super-beings that had all sorts of powers—they might be
strong, telepathic, clairvoyant, all-wise, benevolent, and so
forth; and yet there would still be a sense in which we were
their equals, for we should have our wills and purposes, just
as they had. In order to regard ourselves as wholly inferior,
we should have to be able to conceive of some ability which
somehow transcended the ability to choose, in the same sort
of way that the ability to choose transcends our other abilities, and the abilities of animals: and such a conception
seems impossible. Various religious writers have laid claim
to it, but I have not found any way in which the will of
God, for example, can be intelligibly shown to be a different
sort of will from our own, or more valid than our own—
unless we choose to count it as more valid, which is, of
course, simply to reaffirm the primacy of our own choice
and hence our own will. Since language and its concepts are
based on human choice, they cannot allow any intelligibility
to the notion of a super-choice or a super-will: all such
notions will merely be projections of our own wills in a new
form.

We may use this notion to pick up a point made earlier in
this part. The accidental equality of men depended on the
existence of certain similarities: but the existence of these, as
we saw when considering man and nature, itself depends on a
particular way of looking at the world, the use of particular contexts, and so on. The claim of intrinsic equality
is essentially the claim that every man has an equal ability to
frame his own world-view and his own criteria of similarity.
This claim is a factual one: but it is closely allied to the
claim that every man has also an *equal* right to do this. In
other words, not only does every man *have* a will just as
much as every other man, but also his will *should count for
as much as* the other's. The difficulty of denying this latter
claim is simply that there seems to be no reason *outside* the
wills and criteria of individual men, so to speak, for believing that the will of any one man is superior. It seems
that we have to accept the claim in order to start on any process of argument or morality at all.

Many people may be disposed to accept this outright: but
I think this would be premature. For, again, the *relevance* of

the fact that other people have wills just like my own depends on my own values and criteria. I might think that their wills should not count, because they are stupid or neurotic. It is true that my criteria for stupidity and neurosis are *my* criteria, and may not be shared by them: but then I might think that these facts about them are more important: and to convince me you would have to prove this on my criteria of importance.

There is also another reason of a rather different kind why we cannot step so rapidly from the fact of intrinsic equality to some moral position about human rights. We must not forget that the powers on which we base our intrinsic equality are only actualised by a social environment: in particular, by the human infant being brought up in a society which teaches it a language. Now it would be quite possible for an anti-egalitarian to admit that all adults—let us say more precisely, children over the age of about three or four—had these powers, and hence the rights that went with them: but also to claim that there was no particular reason why we should give these powers to all infants. Thus suppose that for some odd moral reason I prefer a world consisting solely of whites or Aryans, I might treat existing Negroes and non-Aryans with perfect propriety as equals, but refuse to allow Negro or non-Aryan infants to be turned into people by the normal processes of upbringing. In other words, I might accept that people are equals, but fail to see why it should be a good thing to turn infants (or all infants) into people.

We may also remind ourselves of a third objection which is even more radical. Suppose a man's world-view, including his language and criteria of similarity, simply does not take into account the differences between creatures that have wills of their own and creatures that do not. Why should we make the distinctions we make? Why, to put it dramatically, should a super-being from some other galaxy distinguish between men and ants, in the way we want him to distinguish? Is the distinction between intelligent and non-intelligent life one which all intelligent beings are bound to make, and if so what binds them?

These and other difficulties are real ones, although they may seem to us—who share, for the most part, a common outlook and a common language—to be somewhat fantastic.

Earlier we saw that the notion of accidental equality needed to be backed by a more general picture, and the picture painted by intrinsic equality is certainly more general, and may provide more common ground. But it is still not general enough to be as universally convincing as we should wish. For the egalitarian to bring everyone into his fold, he will have to show that everyone's criteria are such that, given due attention to facts and logic, they will be bound to admit the overwhelming importance of intrinsic equality.

PART THREE

EQUALITY
AS A FORMAL
PRINCIPLE

AS I hope will become clear later, the notion of a formal as opposed to a substantial principle is not as plain as some have supposed. Roughly, however, we may say that formal principles are rules which govern, and perhaps actually define, particular types of thinking or symbolic operations. They do not specifically tell you what to think—what the answer is, so to speak—but the rules we try to follow when we do think. 'Stealing is wrong' is a substantial principle; it directs your attention to a particular class of actions, and could by itself effectively influence your behaviour. But 'If you engage in morality, you have to take account of other people' might be a formal principle, tantamount to 'If you don't take account of other people, then you (logically) couldn't be engaged in morality' or 'It wouldn't count as morality if you don't take account of other people'. Similarly 'All objects with mass fall downwards' is a substantial generalisation; but 'Science is a matter of testing hypotheses' might be a formal one, giving you the criteria for scientific thought and activity.

I cannot find a better text for our particular subject than from R. M. Hare's Freedom and Reason :[1] *'Suppose that these people are dividing a bar of chocolate between them, and suppose that they all have an equal liking for chocolate. And let us suppose that no other considerations such as age, sex, ownership of the chocolate, etc., are thought to be relevant. It seems to us obvious that the just way to divide the chocolate is equally. And the principle of universalisability gives us the logic of this conclusion. For if it be maintained that one of the three ought to have more than an equal share, there must be something about his case to make this difference—for otherwise we are making different moral judgements about similar cases. But there is ex hypothesi no relevant difference, and so the conclusion follows. As before it is possible to escape from the conclusion by refraining from making a moral judgement at all; for example, one of the parties may say "I am jolly well going to take the whole bar, and you aren't strong enough to stop me." But, so long as the three are going to make a moral judgement about the way the chocolate ought to be divided, they will have to say, in the circumstances described, that it ought to be divided equally.'*

1. R. M. Hare, *Freedom and Reason* (O.U.P.), pp. 118–19.

I

Universalisability

The principle of universalisability, roughly stated, is that we cannot make different moral judgements about similar cases. We cannot, because if we tried we should find ourselves not making moral judgements at all, but simply expressing our own inclinations or intentions, like the self-willed man in Hare's example. The principle is derived from the logic of moral language; it appears on analysis that words like 'good' are used in conformity with particular sets of descriptive criteria. These criteria may vary from person to person, but each individual in calling something 'good' commends that thing *for* certain characteristics that it has. He is logically bound to describe anything exactly similar as good also. This principle extends beyond the sphere of morality. Thus if there are two pictures very like each other, 'To call one good and the other not commits the speaker to saying that there must be some difference between them which makes them differ in respect of goodness'.[1]

The relevance of this thesis to equality is plain. It suggests some formal basis for the notion of *impartiality*. We cannot have favourites and at the same time claim to be morally justified: for all moral justification must take the form of showing that if we treat one person differently from another there must be a significant difference between the people. To talk of a 'favourite' suggests that there is no significant difference except, as it were, in our own minds. If I give an academic prize to a girl because she scores the highest marks, that is not favouritism, for her superiority

1. ibid., p. 140.

in marks is relevant to prize-giving in an academic context: but if I give her an academic prize just because she is pretty, then I favour her unfairly. We might almost say that 'because' bears two different senses in each case: in the first I am offering a justification by reference to a rule (those with the highest marks get the prizes), whereas in the second I am simply reporting my own feelings (I like giving things to pretty girls).

This principle of impartiality might be expressed in different ways: and the differences will turn out to be important. We might say 'Treat every person the same, unless there is a good reason to treat him differently': or we might say 'Every person's interests (or wants, or inclinations) should count for as much as every other person's, unless there is a good reason why they should not'; or we might say 'Don't favour yourself, or your favourites, at the expense of other people, unless there is a good reason why you should'. These principles would be based on the thesis of universalisability, if indeed they are not versions of them. What we have to do is to consider whether the thesis is true: and if so, what principles it can be made to support.

The first objection that could be made to the thesis is that it seems very difficult to make a clear distinction between the characteristics of the thing one is calling 'good' and one's own feelings: and that there are at least some uses of 'good' where one does not seem to be commending anything that one might reasonably call the characteristics *of a thing*. Thus one might say about eating chocolates 'The second one is never as good as the first', although both the first and second chocolates might in themselves be identical; I might regard someone as a good woman for me to marry, not because of anything about her, but because of something about me (e.g. the fact that I am in love with her).

In reply to the chocolates case, we might say that the characteristics of the two chocolates were different by counting temporal priority as a characteristic; one comes before the other, and hence gives more satisfaction than the other. Similarly we could say that the woman is a 'good person for me to marry' because she has a certain characteristic: namely, the characteristic of inspiring love in me. However, this reduces the principle of universalisability to very slender proportions. For it now appears that it is *logically* possible to commend things for virtually any reason, including the effect they have upon one. Since things that possess the same objective characteristics usually effect a person in the same way, it is of course *psychologically* odd or eccentric to call one example of such a thing good and another example not good. Thus if our criteria for the goodness of pictures is found, so to speak, *in* the picture, then we cannot (logically) call one picture good and an identical picture bad. But if, as in the chocolates case, our criteria are located in our own feelings, being perhaps connected with reactions like boredom, desire for new sensations, etc., then we could perfectly well do this.

Moreover, there are no doubt uses of 'good' which do not imply *any* reason, whether connected with the characteristics of a thing or with our own feelings: as when we say, perhaps of some sensual experience, 'Mm, that's good!', or just ejaculate 'Good!' when we approve of something, or say to a dog 'Good boy!' when it does what we want. This reinforces the conclusion that the thesis is best presented, not so much as a view about how the logic of the word 'good' must, in all instances, necessarily function, but rather as a view about the logic of a particular language-game used by human beings, within which the word 'good' is often used but is not entirely confined.

From one point of view these objections are trivial: but they involve restating the thesis in a significant way. What we now have to say is that there is an important human activity which consists of commending certain *kinds* of things, which must be distinguished from the activity of commending or expressing approval for one *particular* thing. The thesis directs our attention to the context of valuing certain kinds of things, and to the logic of that context. But what does this logic amount to? It comes down to the simple fact that, if we group together certain things as being of the same kind under some rule or other, for the very good reason that these things share certain characteristics which we wish always to commend, then we must stick to the rule, for otherwise it is not really a rule at all. The moral rules I follow may of course be very sophisticated and subtle, hard to state exactly, and admitting of various exceptions. But the exceptions have to be justified. The thesis boils down, there-fore, to an explication of what it is to follow a rule. It would be logically possible, though psychologically hard to envis-age, for a person not to follow moral (and perhaps other) rules at all—that is, for him not to have general principles commending certain *kinds* of things. (Whether or not such a person could use words like 'good' except in atypical ways hardly matters.) What the person cannot do is to claim to be following a rule, and yet refuses to make similar judge-ments on similar cases.

2

Moral Rules and
Other People

If we now return to the possible statements of the principle of impartiality, we can see that there are significant gaps between these statements and the account just given of the thesis of universalisability. In the first place, if we say 'Don't favour yourself at the expense of other people' a person could reject this maxim without falling foul of the universalisability. For the maxim *assumes* that your will and desires are to be counted as similar in importance to those of other people. But you can perfectly well follow rules about the treatment of yourself and others without following *this* rule. The Roman emperor Heliogabalus killed people because he liked to see red blood on green grass. But he has not got to say *either* that 'anyone (even if it be he himself) should be slaughtered, if that is necessary in order to gratify the taste of somebody who likes to see red and green juxtaposed', *or* that he has 'only a selfish desire'.[1] His principle is that you can slaughter people if you are Heliogabalus, or perhaps if you are any Roman emperor. A clearer case still is Shakespeare's Caesar, who, when asked for a reason, says 'The cause is in my will'. This is not the expression of a 'selfish desire', nor of an 'arbitrary' choice in any pejorative sense. If you have a principle that the will of anyone who is Caesar counts as a good reason, then choosing to do what Caesar wills is not arbitrary. The principle itself may be arbitrary, but it is not clear why it should be any more arbitrary than any other principle.

Thus even if we make the notion of impartiality a formal criterion of moral thinking, there is still a significant gap.

1. ibid., p. 170.

Moral thinking follows rules, but it is not necessary to the concept of a rule that it should be inter-personal. One can quite well frame rules for oneself, to assist one in realising a personal ideal: and feelings of conscience or moral obligation, including remorse, regret, guilt, and so forth may attach to these rules as to others. Even if one spent one's life on a desert island it is very probable that one would have rules of this kind. Thus I could frame a rule about not drinking too much coconut wine before I had milked the goats or laid in food for the winter: or about going for a run round the island every day in order to avoid getting fat.

The research of psychologists like Piaget has shown that children first learn to follow rules by obeying or imitating authority, which is generally unquestioned for the first few years of their lives. Later they learn the *point* of following rules by taking part in a social context, such as a game, with other people. Thus the conditions necessary for rule-following would seem to be either authority or some kind of public agreement or convention. We could profitably distinguish between the first type of rule-following, which is a matter of enforced regularity or accepted custom, and the second, which is a matter of the intelligent acceptance, appropriation or inventing of a rule, together with the understanding of when to make exceptions and of the point of the rule. But both these suggest that rules are publicly based, and require the existence of other people—either as authorities in enforcing rules or as partners in framing them. Philosophers following Wittgenstein have also held the view that language, which is essentially a matter of following rules, is necessarily public: briefly, because if we are to be able to speak of using language correctly or incorrectly, there must be a public or external criterion to which we refer. If there is no external rule governing the criteria which an individual might use there would be no sense in which we could say that he was obeying a rule or breaking it.

I do not wish to treat this particular issue in any detail: but it is possible that those who take this line are unduly influenced by the notions of what is 'public' or 'external'. Although in practice we learn nearly all our rules in a social context, the only strictly logical requirement is that there should be an external criterion: and this does not necessarily involve another person, once we remember that the human being is as much a composite entity as an indivisible one. Thus, it is reasonable to suppose, and certainly not logically impossible, that a person should develop a conscience or a super-ego without the assistance of other people, as in the desert-island case. Indeed, it seems probable that the existence of an external reality combined with innate human desires and potentialities suffice for the production of that tripartite division of the self that most people, whether they use Freudian language or not, are accustomed to make: the division between the desires (id), the conscience (super-ego), and the choosing self that mediates between the person and reality (ego).

Granted at least the logical possibility of this, there seems no reason why we should not be able to talk of an 'external' criterion for morality which consists of the individual conscience, unassisted at any stage of its development by other people. Freud talks of the super-ego as introjected people (i.e. the parents), but it could quite well be introjected robots, or introjected wolves, as in the case of Romulus and Remus: and neo-Freudians such as Melanie Klein have traced the origins of the super-ego to factors that operated long before the infant has any conception of a person, and which in fact relate to objects, rather than people, that effect the infant in various ways. Moreover, it is not logically necessary that the *intelligent* following of a rule should be socially learnt, if we insist on interpreting 'socially' by reference to other people rather than simply to the external world. In other words, it is conceivable that a human being could find the necessary criteria for following moral rules, and perhaps rules of language also, as a result of the dialogue between the various parts of his personality on the one hand, and an external reality which does not necessarily include other human beings on the other.

The point can be simply put by saying that I can play a game with rules by myself, such as patience, as well as playing games with other people, such as bridge. Patience is a real game with real rules: I can win, lose and cheat at patience as at bridge. Because it is empirically true that most games are social phenomena, and are taught and learnt in a social context, there is a temptation to suppose that

solo games like patience are logically parasitic upon communal games. But there is no reason to suppose this. It may
well be true that human beings, unlike other creatures, have
the power of inventing games and following rules on their
own: that the capacity to play, to use images as symbols,
and to imitate is a hereditary capacity which only needs
time and the external world to be brought out in the form
of the intelligent application of rules and norms. If this
were not so, indeed, it would be hard to understand how
the general notion of following a rule intelligently could
originally have been acquired at all.

It could of course be argued that in order to obtain the
necessary criteria for moral rules, the individual would have
to accept something *as* a person, or at least as something
on an equality with himself, in the sense that he has to take
it seriously into account when evolving his rule. Thus Romulus and Remus, or Kipling's Mowgli, would only learn rules
by regarding their 'parent' wolves as sources of authority,
and their 'brother' wolves as equals: and if I am on a desert
island, I evolve my rules only by *coming up against* things
like dangerous animals or water-spouts, which I have to
take into account if I am to survive, and indeed which I
might for that very reason be tempted to deify and regard
as gods, spirits, or animistic forces possessed of wills like
my own. But this argument would produce an empty victory: for it would result in modifying the principle of
impartiality—'Treat every person as an equal'—into something like 'Treat everything you *regard as* a person as an
equal'. This would then boil down into the skeletal version
of the universalisability thesis, and amount to saying 'Treat
similar cases similarly'. It would not enable us to make a
distinction between a man who was brought up by human
parents and regarded wolves as subhuman, and a man who
was brought up by wolves and regarded people as sub-
lupine.

In other words, by broadening the universalisability thesis
of treating *similar cases* similarly into the impartiality principle of treating *people* similarly, we are assuming that all
people are, *prima facie*, similar cases. This is a natural assumption, because the application of a common word, 'person', to a number of cases of things in the world suggests

that these cases are in some respects similar. But it is not clear that the respects in which they are similar are the respects which we are compelled to regard as relevant to their treatment. Thus, it is common to men, apes, ostriches, and herons that they have two legs, but this would not normally be a relevant similarity: and conversely, as we argued earlier, a man and a Martian might be different in every respect save that of having the capacity for choice and purpose; yet that similiarity alone might give us good reason for treating men and Martians as equals.

That this not a purely academic point is shown by our own attitude to lunatics, morons, and small children. We do not afford these the same treatment as we afford intelligent and sane adults. It makes little difference whether in defending our conduct we accept the impartiality principle and say that they do not count as 'people', or admit that they are people and thereby reject the impartiality principle. (It would in fact be more in accordance with common usage to take the second alternative.) The point is that the universalisability thesis leaves the question of what counts as a relevantly similar case entirely open, and the impartiality principle does not, and for that reason is more than a formal principle. It asks us to accept as relevant the similarities which we denote, whatever these may be, by the use of the common noun 'person': and as the case of lunatics and morons shows, we do not always feel inclined to give a favourable response to this request.

It is worth noting that the question of who is to count as a person underlies most principles set forth in such concepts as equality, democracy, liberty, natural rights, and so on. There would be no practical value in any assertion about treating every person as an equal, or allowing every person a vote, or maximising the freedom of every person, or saying that every person has certain rights, if we allow ourselves a completely free hand in saying who counts as a person. 'Government by the people' is an empty phrase if we refuse to count slaves, women, Negroes, or Jews as people.

Even these objections, however, might be thought trivial. They amount to saying that the concept of a moral rule is not logically dependent on, or reducible to, regarding other people on a par with oneself; first, because there can be moral rules without the existence of other people at all; and secondly, because one does not have to regard other people as *people*. But it might be said that, although one could have rules which did not give parity to other people, and which could yet give some kind of rational justification for one's actions, they would not be *moral* rules and the justification would not be a *moral* justification.

Are moral rules by definition those which afford parity to others? This is in a sense simply a question about our use of 'moral', but it is nevertheless not a trivial question. First, it seems that the man on a desert island whose conscience troubles him if he drinks too much or gets fat does have moral rules: that is, he has rules which are backed by the authority of conscience and which have the same 'feel' as inter-personal moral rules. We should be at a loss to know how to describe them if not by the word 'moral'. So it seems that *other* people do not have to be involved. Secondly, a king or absolute ruler might acknowledge no one as on a par with himself, and yet have moral rules about how he treated his subjects. He might not regard those subjects as people in the fullest sense, any more than we would regard complete lunatics or morons as people; yet he would feel a moral duty towards them, just as we feel a moral duty towards lunatics and morons (and, for that matter, towards animals). So it seems that other *people* do not have to be involved either.

Now we could argue that these are nevertheless cases in which we grant parity to others in principle, even if not in practice. We could represent the desert islander as saying 'I—and therefore anyone in my position—ought not to get drunk or grow too fat'; and the king as saying 'I—and any other king in a similar position—must carry out certain duties towards my subjects'. But this argument reduces us again to the skeletal version of universalisability—the simple thesis that similar cases call for similar judgements. If the desert islander or the king is following a rule of behaviour, from which he can derive the proposition that he ought to act in certain ways, then he must also agree that an exactly similar situation involving similar people calls for the same judgement. We have done no more—though this is important enough—than repeat the distinction between judging according to a rule, and merely expressing a selfish desire or a pang of conscience.

We have seen that the principle of impartiality is a substantial principle, and needs to be justified by something more than the thesis of universalisability; but we have so far taken it for granted that the thesis of universalisability itself is not open to question. Nor is it so open, provided it is kept as a strictly formal principle. We have to remember that an imperative sentence such as 'Treat like cases alike' only *looks* like a substantial demand. The sense is really that of a conceptual or linguistic explication, amounting to a description of what it *means* to follow a rule or to give a rational justification: from which alone, of course, nothing of substance follows. We might just as well say 'Treat dissimilar cases dissimilarly', or more fully 'Treat everybody differently unless you have good reason to believe that they are the same in some relevant respect'. These are simply reminders to us to consider the rules on which we are supposed to be basing our judgements and our treatment: a reminder that, in framing a rule, we have *ipso facto* accepted some characteristics as relevant and others as irrelevant.

3

Rules and Ideals

We have considered the difficulties involved in closing the gap between this formal principle and a particular substantial principle, the principle of impartiality: but we ought also to consider the difficulty of closing the gap *at all*. For if we are to close it, it seems necessary to assume that we have some substantial rules—either the rules of impartiality and liberal morality in general, or others—which, when taken in conjunction with the formal principle, will produce results. This difficulty is a very radical one. If I accept that Negroes are relevantly similar to whites, and have a rule about treating whites in a certain way, then I am logically bound to treat Negroes similarly. But if you were going through this process of argument with me, I might question two points. First, I might deny the similarity of the Negroes: and this represents the difficulty of moving from the universalisability thesis to the particular substantial principle of impartiality. But secondly, I might refuse to have any substantial rules about the treatment of whites, so that it becomes a matter of indifference whether I care to regard Negroes as similar to them or no.

This may seem an implausible case: but it points to a vast area of uncertainty. We commonly assume that following rules consistently—perhaps we should rather say simply 'following rules'—is a good thing. Certainly it would be hard to conceive of a human being who did not follow *some* rules —the laws of logic and the rules governing the particular language he spoke would be obvious examples. But it is not at all clear just *how much* consistency or rule-following ought to be done, particularly in the sphere of morality and personal choice. What happens in practice is that we assume the importance of consistency in following those rules which we ourselves approve, those which we take seriously. But this seems to give us no better basis for answering our questions than the basis of what is commonly accepted as morally serious, which seems somewhat insecure.

Thus, if a tyrant killed people without justifying this by reference to a rule, but just because he felt like it, we should describe this as 'arbitrary' in a pejorative sense. But if I choose to go for a walk, or to take out a particular girl, or to read a particular book, it is not usually demanded of me that I justify this by a rule. Since 'arbitrary' is so often pejorative, we might call this behaviour 'spontaneous'. It is not at all clear by what criterion we distinguish these two sorts of cases; and it is perhaps worth pointing out that there are many people, particularly amongst the young, who follow a quasi-coherent 'philosophy' or way of life that is notoriously and deliberately less rule-governed than others.

It is not simply a question of *what* rules to frame in a particular area nor even of *how many* rules to frame or *to what extent* behaviour should be rule-governed. It can be a question of whether to have any rules in a particular area *at all*. For instance, extreme liberals might hold that no rules whatsoever should govern sexual morality. It is at this point that we begin to wonder whether if one area can be left totally ungoverned by rules all areas might not be: and to wonder what in general is the point of having rules. This is the context in which certain writers might plausibly advocate some form of total irrationalism, which in the field of morality produces such assertions as 'A man's morals are his own business', or 'It's just a matter of how you feel'. This general attitude has long since prevailed in the matter of religion, in which it is felt that 'Either you believe something or you don't', and that questions of truth do not really arise.

It would be both natural and correct to reply to any challenge offered by some form of fundamental irrationalism by pointing out that rules are necessary in order to fulfil human aims, purposes and plans. We might justifiably accuse some of those who object to rules *a priori* of being bewitched by the idea that rules are always in a bad sense restrictive, or that they diminish the possibilities of individual expression. If your rules are framed with reference to carrying out a particular purpose, they are not only restrictive, but essential. If you want to get the right answer to a sum, or build a bridge, or mend a car, you have to attend to the rules of mathematics and science: these rules enlarge the individual's capabilities rather than restrict them. The same applies to the fields of morals and art and all other purposive activities, though the rules governing these will be of a different kind.

Yet there is still a possible line of defence for the irrationalist. He might say that it was precisely of excessive purposiveness and desire to plan that he was complaining. Why must we suppose that every part, or even any part, of our lives should be directed towards some end of the achievement of some purpose? After all, there *are* cases when we do things 'just because we feel like it': as we might say, 'just for the experience'. It is not necessary to regard life as a series of problems to be solved by the application of rules, or as an attempt to get from A to B quickly and efficiently; we might just as well regard it as a kind of casual stroll during which various experiences befall us. We should not seek out such experiences, but simply let them happen.

Of course the practical impossibility of taking this view to its limits is plain. There are certain purposes and aims which we can hardly help having: among these are the necessities of food, shelter, health, and the avoidance of pain and intolerable suffering. Our purposes, in other words, are (partly, at least) based on wants which are inevitable features of human nature. It may be that we are often over-purposive, or that we all ought to lead more relaxed lives, or that we ought not to plan with such desperate earnestness: some such thesis as this may well be plausible. But the notion of a totally purposeless existence, an existence in which we have no desires to drive us to seek certain ends, seems absurd. We might still ask, however, whether it is *necessarily* absurd: could we not envisage some such existence as that of the Buddhist conception of Nirvana, in which desire is totally absent: or perhaps a life of complete contemplation untroubled by any desire, such as philosophers frequently recommend?

Before trying to answer this question, it will be as well to stop and take stock of the general direction in which the argument is driving us. What has happened is that, in order to seek some general form of justification either for following a particular type of rule, such as the liberal principles of impartiality and equality, or for following rules at all, we find ourselves referring to human ends and purposes, and thus to certain general ways of life or *ideals*. We were driven from a consideration of a specific or substantial principle of equality to a consideration of a general, formal principle which indeed promised to be no less important. But we were then forced to consider how this formal principle could be justified: or rather, since it is a conceptual explication rather than a principle that anyone is trying to sell us, to consider how valuable, in practice, such a principle could be. And this turns out to depend on how far, if at all, we propose to adopt a life which is rule-governed.

However hard it may be to get beyond this point, it seems that *something* has to be said to meet the situation in which we now find ourselves. Perhaps I can make this plain by borrowing again from Hare, who writes: 'If somebody wants to send himself and his whole family to the gas-chamber simply on the ground that they are descended from people with hooked noses, is there, or could there possibly be, any moral philosophy that could argue with him?'[1]

The moral philosopher need not be disturbed 'by the logical possibility of people becoming fanatics without self-contradiction'. Hare is undisturbed because his aim is not 'to produce a watertight method of argument'. The layman would perhaps not demand a watertight method: but he would certainly demand some rational criterion for dealing with fanatics—or perhaps some rational criterion which justifies calling them fanatics.

Most people who hold radically different moral views from the liberalism which is still fashionable in the western world do so because they are different from us and live in a different sort of world. When they argue along the lines laid down by Hare, they may (like Sartre's anti-semite)[2] be only

1. ibid., p. 172.
2. J. P. Sartre, 'Portrait of the Anti-Semite' (in W. Kaufmann's *Existentialism from Dostoevsky to Sartre*)

pretending to argue, offering their arguments as a sop either to liberals in other countries or to that part of themselves which wants to play the game liberals play. They have *decided to be different people*. If we cannot offer any rational criteria by which their decision can be counted as mistaken, we cannot rest content with saying merely that it is fortunate that there are so few of them. For why is it fortunate? Whence do we derive the pejorative implication of 'fanatic'?

These differences might be described as the result of different ideals: but the word 'ideals' may be misleading here. We might also describe them, with more vagueness but less chance of unjustifiably excluding some important question, as the result of different pictures of what human personality is or ought to be. It is not the question 'What shall I do?' which we have to answer if we are fully to underwrite our morality, but some such question as 'What shall I be?' This is a much more difficult question, not least because the meaning of the question is not clear, and it is consequently unclear what would count as an answer. At this stage, however, I am only anxious to outline the many *kinds* of difficulties into which we are led by trying to justify moral thinking in general, and a liberal morality in particular.

Thus even granted a liberal morality, whereby we have to take account of our own and other people's interests, we must first be able to identify an interest as forming part of a person. I have to identify my interest (my wants and future wants) as *mine*: this will depend on the way in which I have answered the general question 'What shall I be?' On the answer to this, in all probability, will depend the answer to questions about what to count as somebody else's interests. Thus we might say that a man's interests are what he *says* he wants, or what he seems disposed to try to get. But this itself is to adopt a certain picture of human personality which is questionable: we ourselves would feel tempted to drop such a picture when dealing with cases like the drug addict, who says he wants only his drug and always tries to get it, but whom we restrain, according to Hare, 'in his own interests'.[1] We often renege in such cases by talking about his 'true wants' or 'real interests'; but now either these phrases import our own moral ideals from elsewhere, and

1. ibid., p. 174.

hence forbid us to use interest as a criterion for moral judgement, or else they rely on painting a new picture of human
personality which itself needs to be justified. (This is why
non-liberals feel liberal principles to be somehow *bogus*, i.e.
covertly dependent on ideals which the principles themselves
cannot justify.) If we do not renege in cases like drug addic-
tion or (worse) suicide, we still have to face a general question about what is to count as a person. We can take what
a person says he wants, or any other factual criterion we like,
as indicative of his interests; but are children people? What
about pygmies, morons, Martians and psychopaths? Are
neurotics people only when they are not being neurotic?
Can we count indoctrinated Communists along with zombies
and lunatics? These are not just questions about the normal
use of words like 'person' or 'rational entity'. No doubt we
have criteria for this, but on what are these criteria based?

Even assuming one could formulate a principle about
not overriding the interests of others, which anybody would
always be prepared to abide by, and which was not circu-
larly formulated in terms of 'best interests', this formulation
would be the result of an ideal: and Hare does not think that
one can argue conclusively about ideals, e.g. as between that
of the ascetic and that of the *bon vivant*.[1] To treat people as
ends in themselves is the product of an ideal: it is surely a
clear case of a principle formulated as a result of asking
what I and other people should *be*—in this case, roughly,
equals as opposed to masters or slaves. Again, one would
naturally suppose it scandalous if there were not some
reason for adopting this ideal; but it could not be supported
by reference to the principle of considering the interests
of others, since the principle is itself derived from the ideal.

1. ibid., p. 151.

4

Equality and Liberalism

In Part One we observed that one of the egalitarian's first demands was for impartiality of treatment. He insists that social arrangements should be rule-governed: that there should be laws and social principles, impartially applied, which override the arbitrary will of the authorities. But now it appears very doubtful whether we have any firm criteria for deciding what is 'arbitrary' or what is 'impartial'. No doubt everyone would willingly agree that there should be rules: but they would not agree on what sort of rules should be established, or how many of them there ought to be. The notion of impartiality, as a purely formal principle, gives the egalitarian no help.

Nor would he be satisfied if it did. For the way of life most egalitarians wish to advocate, which might be fairly described as the liberal way of life, rests on far more than the notion of impartiality. He desires at least two more things: democracy and liberty. It is important to see how these derive from his belief that intrinsic equality, as we described it in Part Two, should be regarded not only as a metaphysical truth about human beings, but as an operative political principle. Intrinsic equality suggests that the wills, choices and values of each man are as valid as those of any other man. The notion of equality of scope, or equality of power in decision-making, obviously follows from this: and hence he is led to a belief in democracy. But more than this: for his belief is not properly represented by saying that the will of one man, as it were, *weighs as much* as the will of another, as if we were entitled to judge the weight of both by some external criterion. That would allow him to support democracy, but no more. His belief is rather that we *are not entitled to weigh the wills of other men by our own criteria at all*. Hence he will not believe that a majority has any absolute right to dictate to an individual: for him, the overriding of any individual's will—even if he be in a minority of one—will always be regrettable. Thus he is led to a belief in liberty.

I want now to show that these liberal notions are just as empty and incoherent as the notion of impartiality, and hence that we must accept two conclusions (1) that it is the notion of intrinsic equality which gives sense to these other liberal notions, and not vice versa, and consequently (2) that unless we can defend intrinsic equality we cannot defend the others. In other words, it is our failure so far to see *why* a belief in intrinsic equality is a necessary moral belief— our failure to defend intrinsic equality as an ideal of practical living—that makes nonsense of many of our liberal assumptions.

Liberals from J. S. Mill onwards have attempted to produce a criterion for law-making which is free from moral bias: indeed which is precisely designed to disqualify any particular moral view, even that of a majority in a society, from acting as such a criterion. Roughly, the criterion is designed to allow the will of every individual full scope, unless it interferes with, affects or harms other individuals. (It seems plausible to frame this criterion in terms of interfering rather than in terms of affecting or harming. 'Affect' is too wide to cover the relevant cases, and 'harm' too narrow: thus all, or at least far too many, actions affect other people, and by putting you under temporary hypnosis, without your knowledge, I am not harming you, though I am certainly depriving you of your liberty.) We say, then, that the authorities are only allowed to interfere with the individual when the individual himself interferes with another. About this I want to make two points which perhaps add up to the same general point, though they are worth considering individually:

(a) If this were a criterion only of law-making, it would be useless or worse than useless. There is no point in refusing to make a law against Jews, Negroes, homosexuals, etc. if they are attacked by a lynch mob instead: and there is not much point in stopping this if society is going to refuse them employment or intermarriage, spit at them in the streets, and so on. So what the liberal must really be doing is to claim that there are only certain ways in which anybody can legitimately treat anyone else; he is arguing for the correctness of a certain kind of human contact, a certain context of communication—roughly, one in which I respect your wants as much as my own, and do not use force, threats, or any kind of pressure. Moreover, he has *either* to say that no other kind of contact is ever legitimate, *or* to define clearly and without the use of his own moral values what exceptions can be made. In other words, the consistent liberal has to take care of cases which some early liberals were content to leave to the moral pressures of society, convention, or right-thinking people: and since these cases would include not only pimps, opium addicts, and suicides, but also children, students, neurotics, and the many occasions when we feel justified in treating sane adults by something other than pure reason, we want to know how the consistent liberal does this.

(b) The real difficulty with the criterion of interference is that what is interference to one man is not to another. Suppose I am made physically ill by the presence of Jews or Negroes, or by certain types of sexual behaviour. Plainly this interferes with me. All that a tyrannical people has to do, therefore, is to react violently enough to something: liberals then seem bound to count that thing as interference, and admit laws and other forms of pressure to prevent it. No doubt this in itself is not fatal: even the most liberal liberals would pass a law against racial integration, if the only alternative was a lynch mob. But they would do so only with reluctance: and what justifies the reluctance? There is now a temptation to say that there must be something wrong with those who are interfered with by the presence of Jews and Negroes. But this seems to reintroduce some kind of moral judgement, which is cheating.

One way out of this suggests itself. We can distinguish between things which people cannot help finding intolerable, such as pain, death, physical bondage, brain-washing, etc., and things which we could reasonably count as prejudice or sheer intolerance, such as dislike of Jews and Negroes. Then we say, not that the prejudices of the second class are morally justifiable or unjustifiable, but simply that they are politically a pity: because we all want to be able to do as much of what we want as possible, so that the more invulnerable we are to the effects of other people the better. From this angle it would be very convenient if I did not mind being hurt or sexually assaulted, for then sadists and others could do what they wanted. There would be difficult cases, caused by the difficulty of what counts as being able to help finding things tolerable. Thus it is not clear whether my dislike of sexual assault is to count as a silly but deep-rooted prejudice, which I could jettison if I went to a psychoanalyst for three years, or as something which is part of my basic nature, like my liability to pain. But the liberal could still sustain an ultimate ideal of the perfect citizen as an invulnerable, non-impingeable-on person, and claim that we ought to work towards that.

What the liberal is arguing for here is for the kind of people, and the kind of social arrangements, that allow the maximum expression of desire with the minimum of im-pinging on others. This amounts to what sociologists call the institutionalisation of conflicts: and the snag is that it is possible that some conflicts logically cannot be institution-alised. Thus if I can work off all my aggression by playing football, in which not too many people get hurt, that is no doubt a gain: and if my aggression can only be satisfied by other people's pain, if my wants precisely *are* to hurt people, no doubt in principle we could build people who did not mind being hurt. But that would take all the fun out of sadism: and the real difficulty is if my wants precisely are to frustrate your wants. We could, perhaps, by conditioning or indoctrination, change you so that you did not mind your wants being frustrated, but then the whole point of liberalism collapses, since its argument here rests on the premise that people ought to be able to do what they want as much as possible.

In any case it seems, in practice, that the liberal must face the question of whether some wants can reasonably be counted as more legitimate or more rational than others. His dilemma is this: Suppose a society in which the wants of the majority are sadistic, and suppose that they are prepared to universalise these wants in the form of moral principles or ideals. Now he can, first, to quote from Hare, arbitrate 'between people's interests and ideals and give as much weight to each person's as to any other's',[1] respecting the ideals of others as he does his own. But if he does this (a) he cannot defend the minority of non-sadists in the way he has been trying to, and (b) it is not clear that his thesis deserves the name of liberalism, since it seems to consist entirely of accepting the wants of the majority as valid however illiberal those wants may be. (It is doubtful whether anyone who calls himself a liberal would in fact assent to this course.) Secondly, he can fight the sado-masochists tooth and nail on the liberal grounds that their wants interfere with the wants of others: but now the sadists will represent what the liberals call interference as due to prejudice on the part of the non-sadists and therefore not genuine interference (just as the liberal does not count intense dislike produced by Jews as genuine interference), and how can the liberal prove them wrong without some moral critera?

The mere fact that, in what we call civilised societies, we often agree about what are legitimate wants or genuine cases of intereference is, of course, unhelpful: though it is this which makes it plausible for Hare and others to talk about those that disagree as fanatics. But someone like Nietzsche, for example, would claim that this agreement merely represents the fanaticism of a majority which irrationally hates things like cruelty, violence, and rape, and has subtly managed to indoctrinate its children so that they no longer want, or think they want, such things. This seems to me a very plausible view, and is certainly logically possible.

The concept of democracy is liable to substantially the same objections, though these are here more obvious than in the case of liberty. Democracy is no doubt something to do with government by the people, but what is to count as 'the people'? The ancient Athenians excluded slaves and women from the right to vote: other states have disqualified criminals, lunatics, morons, Negroes, and those under twenty-one. We cannot say that slaves, women, etc. are not people, in the normal sense of the word: but it is still universally believed that there are some people whose wills should not count, and who should therefore not count as citizens. We

1. ibid., p. 178.

describe them as 'irrational', 'mad', 'not capable of thinking for themselves', 'uneducated', and so forth. Here again we seem to be imposing our own moral views under a very thin disguise. For it is not clear that we have any reason for disqualifying these classes of people *other than* simply that they would form opinions of which we would disapprove. But if we give ourselves a completely free hand in disqualifying certain groups of people as citizens, then it is open to us to go as far as we like in restricting the electorate, whilst still representing our political system as democratic. If we exclude morons, why not exclude all those with an I.Q. of under 100? Or under 150? If we exclude lunatics, why not neurotics?

What we have shown is not simply that there are a few difficult cases which embarrass the liberal, but that the concepts of liberty and democracy are vacuous unless backed by a particular picture of what wants, desires or behaviour are reasonable or legitimate. There is no doubt that liberals in the western world, including liberal philosophers, do have such a picture; but it is not clearly delineated, and rarely defended. This may be partly because many philosophers confine themselves to explicating, as we have been trying to explicate, the notion of impartiality as a formal principle, and leave the defence of particular ways of life to other thinkers and writers. This division of labour may be desirable. But it is bound to create one of two regrettable impressions: either that concepts like equality, liberty, and democracy can be shown to be intelligible and defensible by purely formal considerations, or—once we have seen through this—that they are not ultimately defensible at all, so that it becomes a matter of arbitrary choice whether one believes in the liberal way of life or not.

Some parallels may clarify this point. Most people would agree that tolerance is a good thing. But tolerance is a vacuous notion unless we already know what sort of things we are supposed to tolerate and what not to tolerate. To a Protestant the Roman Catholics are 'intolerant' because they do not approve of mixed marriages, to a Polynesian the Anglo-Saxons are 'intolerant' because they do not approve of nakedness or premarital intercourse and so on. Now it is plain that a purely formal examination of the concept of toleration will not help here: nothing much will be gained by asking what it *means* to be tolerant. For the meaning of 'tolerant', like the meaning of 'strict', 'reasonable', 'fair', 'unbiassed', 'moderate', and many other words, derives chiefly from a particular context in which certain values are taken for granted. In the same way one can call a political party or a newspaper 'moderate' or 'middle of the road' only because there exist other parties and newspapers which are 'extremist'. If you have a scale with Communism at one end and Fascism at the other, then of course you can call some of the parties who come in the middle of the scale 'moderate': and if you range your newspapers in an order which begins with the *Daily Worker* at one extreme and some very right-wing papers at the other, then no doubt you can describe *The Times* (or even *Time Magazine*) as 'unbiassed'. But a Communist or a Fascist would naturally have quite a different scale.

Yet we are left with the feeling that these liberal notions do, after all, say *something*. The difficulty is to give an interpretation of what they say which is not simply an endorsement of our own moral values, and yet is not merely vacuous. Liberals, just as much as others, very often smuggle in their own values and desires under the guise of some general principle which they assume everyone accepts, and it is this sort of smuggling which we have been endeavouring to detect in this Part. There remains the task of giving a more positive and defensible interpretation to equality and the other liberal notions which it sustains.

PART FOUR

EQUALITY
AS AN IDEAL

I

Rationality
and Choice

Why should we choose liberal or egalitarian values, rather than other values? Part of the answer to this question will consist of giving a clearer picture than we have so far given of what egalitarian values actually are, or what it really is that liberals advocate when they talk about liberty, equality, and democracy. But an equally essential part of the answer will consist in examining why we in general should choose one value rather than another: and though this raises what is perhaps the central and most difficult problem in moral philosophy, we must try to tackle it first.

A question like 'Why should I choose one value (or way of life) rather than another?' when posed in this general form, may seem unanswerable or even unintelligible. For (we may say) if I thus place myself outside the whole realm of value, there is no force in the word 'should'; there can be no sense in saying that I *should* or that I *ought* to choose one value rather than another, unless I already have some values which will give point to these words. To students of British empirical philosophy this is most familiar as a thesis derived from the work of Hume and G. E. Moore: briefly, that facts do not logically entail values, and that you cannot derive an 'ought' from an 'is'. The thesis is too familiar to need stating at great length here. It is purely logical thesis, derived from the distinction between descriptive and evaluative language, and may be accepted as such: but we must be careful to distinguish it from some quite different view about the ultimate arbitrariness or irrationality of value.

If we look at extreme cases of moral irrationality, we can see that they are in some respects similar to arbitrary reasons in general. The fact that today is Monday is not a reason for killing someone, any more than it is a reason for believing that the earth is round or that two and two are four. Anybody can choose to count it as a reason, and could create and follow a system of rules based on such pseudo-reasons, but his choice would not be rational because his rules would not be related to his subject-matter. Today being Monday has nothing to do with morality, any more than with science or mathematics. Such a person would not know what morality was. Morality is precisely a set of rules based on human desires as its subject-matter: not necessarily other people's desires, but some desires. Nor is it based solely on desires in the sense of consciously adopted wants, intentions or choices: it is based on human nature. It is of course logically open for a man not to bother about having any rules to do with controlling or finding satisfaction for his own nature, but that (I shall argue) would be to resign from being a human being.

It thus seems more hopeful, at least, to start with some such question as 'Why should I choose one way of life rather than another?', for there seems to be a possibility of finding an answer—to put it dramatically—in the content of the word 'I': that is, in the nature of the person who asks the question. Part of the answer does indeed lie here. Human beings find themselves with certain desires and purposes, such as the desire to eat or to avoid pain. The existence of these desires and purposes is a good enough *prima facie* reason for consciously intending, planning or choosing to carry them out. Asked to justify my eating or avoiding pain, I can perfectly well reply 'Because I'm hungry' or 'Because it hurts'. Our desires and wants, likes and dislikes, form the basis, and hence the starting-point, of our moral thinking. It would be odd, to the point of irrationality, to give such replies as 'Because I dislike it' or 'Because that's just what I don't want to do'. Of course there are plenty of occasions where we may deny ourselves the fulfilment of one purpose or desire: but then we should naturally do this in order to satisfy some other purpose or desire, which would in some way be connected with our natures. To allow ourselves to invent totally disconnected purposes—to produce moral criteria out of the blue, so to speak—would be to allow ourselves to give reasons like those mentioned above, such as 'Because it's Monday' or 'Because my name begins with W'.

Human beings have the power to make their own natures: to change their wants and desires. We may cut a long story short by supposing, as it is not too futuristic to suppose, that we had the technical ability to create rational entities to our own specification: we can give them whatever personalities, desires and feelings we choose. (This is in fact merely an extreme case of a situation which already confronts us, e.g. when we form the personalities of our children or when by brain-surgery and drugs we are able to change the character of another person.) In this situation have we any reason to build in one set of desires rather than another or to set up one sort of relationship rather than another between the conscious ego of the entity and its character? This suggests that behind the question 'Why should I choose one way of life rather than another?' lies the even more radical question—so radical that it may sound vacuous—'What shall I be?'

Some existentialist philosophers (so far as I understand them) hold that the answers to these questions must be a matter of arbitrary decision, and that it is possible for us, even saddled with the desires we have, to 'choose in abstraction'. But this seems to be a mistake: I think an important one. The mistake is more obvious if we consider notions like having an aim, a purpose, or a plan. These notions are plainly unintelligible without bringing in the idea of a desired end or objective: they must (logically) be consciously or unconsciously motivated. When I plan I intend to take certain steps towards an end. In the cases of choosing or intending or deciding to do something there may be no intervening steps: and this creates the illusion that choice can be dissociated from desire. But if I choose to do something I must in some sense want to do it. One's desires may be immediate rather than long-term, but they must be present for a genuine and deliberate choice to be made. If they were not, one would simply *find oneself* doing something. We might almost say that to choose something *is* to regard that thing as an end, or as a means to an end: and no doubt there are reasons, conscious or unconscious, why we regard things as ends. Either something moves me to choose, or else I choose for a conscious purpose. To put the point in a different way, it is possible to build a machine that selects: but it is not (logically) possible to build a selector mechanism that selects *on no principles whatsoever*. You programme it (give it criteria of value) to select some things and reject others. If it had no criteria at all, it would not be *selecting*: the situation would rather be as if it had some kind of nervous twitch.

What follows is tentative, but seems to flow naturally from taking the question 'What shall I be?' seriously. The questioner, by virtue of his question, seems to cede two points: first, that he wants to be, that he (in some sense) accepts life and does not wish to resign from the whole game: and, second, that some answers to the question would be more justifiable than others. This precludes him from saying, either 'I shan't be anything at all', or 'One way of life is as good as another'. What we have got, then, is a living and choosing entity who is in serious doubt about how to model himself. This suggests that the criteria we offer him should connect in some way with the notions of being alive (being an animate creature), of choosing rationally or justifiably, and of being in a good position to settle doubts.

Now extreme cases of irrationality, such as the fanatics quoted by Hare, or the man who replies 'Because it's Monday', seem very close to cases of insanity or near-insanity: and this suggests that the criteria we need are connected with the criteria for sanity. It is a further encouragement that we can here produce a sense for 'rational' which is not the sense of 'rule-governed' but rather the sense of 'sane' or 'reasonable'. The sense of 'rule-governed', as we saw in the last Part, will not meet our situation, because (briefly) it is open to a person to be governed by what rules he likes. However, two difficulties face us. First, the normal criteria for sanity or reasonableness still leave a very wide choice open to the man who asks 'What shall I be?' There are many differences of moral opinion, and many different ways of seeing oneself, this side of what we commonly call insanity. Second, we must be careful that the criteria of sanity (a) are not morally loaded in favour of our own or our society's opinions, for that would make our argument circular: and (b) do not amount to saying that 'sane' means merely typical, usual, or (in the descriptive sense) normal, for if that is all it means then we have offered no kind of inducement to be sane.

It is the difficulty of meeting this point which has inspired philosophers such as Nietzsche to write in such a way that they appear to prefer the mad to the sane, and theorists such as D. H. Lawrence to condemn the reason of the 'reasonable man' in favour of some instinctive or spontaneous approach to life. The point could be alternatively put by asking whether those whom we call mad are really mad; or whether the 'reasonable man' who figures so prominently in jurisprudence and even in moral philosophy is really reasonable. What worries those who are, perhaps, of a naturally rebellious or critical turn of mind is that the criteria of sanity and reasonableness are merely the criteria of the prevailing establishment in disguise.

Demands to 'be reasonable' are in practice rarely tantamount merely to demands to consider the facts, use one's imagination, stifle prejudice, and so on, to which we should all assent: very often they amount to demands to accept the *status quo*, or to accept a particular way of doing things. What is 'reasonable' in terms of British politics, in so far as they are conducted by the 'Athenaeum method' described by C. P. Snow,[1] is not 'reasonable' in Moscow, Pekin, or South Africa. Whether certain ways of doing political and other business are, in a higher and better sense, more reasonable than others is a very open question, the answer to which would turn partly on the particular position of that society at a particular time. But this sense of 'reasonable' is rarely examined. The test is, of course, whether the individual is being asked to be reasonable in terms of *his own* ends and purposes, or in terms of somebody else's. If a boy wants to leave school and has nothing to gain by staying, it it reasonable only in the establishment's term for him to work hard and behave well: but if he wants to get a good report or pass an examination, it is reasonable in his own terms also.

There is also the feeling that although a particular way of doing business involves virtues to which, in the abstract, we should assent—calmness, patience, willingness to talk things

1. C. P. Snow, *Science and Government.*

over, etc.—yet somehow there may be vital things which are left unsaid or unexpressed. Certain passionate feelings or desires ought to come out: and if the context of communication, reasonable though it may appear if we omit these feelings and desires, makes no allowances for them, we may hold that they had better come out in a violent or 'unreasonable' way rather than not at all (there are times when one *ought* to lose one's temper). This too leads the irrationalist to suppose that it is not always a good thing to be reasonable: or even, if he is prepared to go so far, to be sane. We still have to face the difficulty, therefore, of providing some kind of criteria which will commend themselves, not just to the sane or reasonable man (for that would be to argue in a circle), but to any man who is prepared to ask some such question as 'What shall I be? or 'What sort of personality should I have?'

I think these difficulties can be met by pushing our criteria for sanity beyond their normal limits, and presenting them in such a way that our questioner finds it necessary to meet them because of what his question itself concedes. First let us consider four cases:

1 The man whose consciousness or ego has lost touch with and control over his desires, and who hence cannot inspect them, order them, or choose between them. Such a man might be said to lack proper *communication* within himself. In an extreme case, where his ego was a battleground of contending forces rather than a stage whereon the *dramatis personae* were controlled by a producer or director, he would certainly count as mad.

2 The man who lacks any *intensity* of desire. Mild cases would count as apathy or listlessness, severer cases as extreme depression, and when the stage of total apathy or lifelessness was reached we might begin to use words like 'insane'.

3 The man who has a perpetual *conflict* of desires. He would normally count as 'neurotic' rather than lunatic, but when the conflict reached a certain point, as perhaps in schizophrenia, we should call him mad.

4 The man whose desires are *narrow* or *exclusive* like the case of the opium addict or fanatic: these count as mad if the narrowness is great enough.

These criteria are not morally loaded, at least in the sense that we have not said that some desires are better than others. Nor have we said that one particular order of the mind is to be preferred to another: only that order rather than disorder—communication rather than fragmentation—is part of our concept of sanity. We could conceive of Martians with quite different desires and values, and still be able to make a distinction between mad or sane Martians.

The four cases above yield criteria which might recommend themselves to anyone who, like our questioner, wants both to be in a good position to settle his doubts, and to be a person. It would be possible to make our criteria logically necessary for him, by refusing to count him as a person unless they were met in a very high degree. (One might plausibly say that a schizophrenic was, in a significant sense, not one person but two.) Yet it would be a mistake to do this, not just because it does violence to the normal use of 'person' (neurotics are plainly people), but because we should have won a barren victory: our questioner might reasonably say that his question does not commit him to wanting to be a person in our (new) sense. Nevertheless, we might reasonably be encouraged to frame these four criteria in terms of (a) good communication within the personality, (b) intensity of desire, (c) harmony of desire, and (d) breadth or variety of desire: for since when any of these criteria are very badly satisfied we call the person mad, we might hope that they represent a principle or principles of living to which all of us, including our questioner, actually subscribe.

There seem to be two reasons why these criteria seem inevitable for any living and choosing entity:

1 For any such entity 'life' inevitably consists of desire and the satisfaction of desire, of the achievement of ends and purposes, of goal-directed activities. This is a logical truth: it would not be logically possible to make genuine choices (as we saw earlier), or to be anything like what we normally call a person, if one abdicated from the whole realm of desire and satisfaction. To prefer life to death, therefore, is to accept the *general* notions of satisfaction and achievement. To this minimum our questioner has committed himself by his question.

But it is not immediately obvious why this should commit

him to seeking as much satisfaction as possible. He may take advantage or an ambiguity in 'satisfaction'. He may accept that any desires he has should be (fully) satisfied, but not accept that he should have more and stronger desires whose fulfilment would bring him 'more satisfaction'. Either desires are satisfied or they are not: and why should he not choose to have weak satisfied desires rather than strong satisfied desires? Yet besides the sense of 'satisfaction' which is solely related to existing desires, there is also a sense which is not: the sense brought out when we say that a person who has no desire for (say) food or music is 'missing something' or 'not leading a full life'. Moreover, none of us would turn down the chance of increased satisfaction in this sense, other things being equal. This last is an important proviso: for in practical decisions there might be all sorts of good reasons for turning it down; for instance, to generate and satisfy the new desire might involve frustrating other desires. But if we assume a *carte blanche* situation in which other things are equal, our choices would suggest that we do subscribe to some such principle.

It is not a logical truth that if life is worth living, it is worth living to the full. But it becomes a logical necessity if our acceptance of life is such as to commit us to a rule that more life is always to be preferred to less: and we do in fact seem to follow some such rule. Thus if our questioner wants to live at all, he is likely to think it better to be a pig than a cabbage, and better to be Socrates than a pig: and he must also think it better to be a super-Socrates, with more satisfied desires and greater awareness, than just to be Socrates. He would want 'to have life, and have it more abundantly', because there would be a general characteristic about life which he wants to maximise, namely satisfaction in the wider sense. Conversely, if he refused to acknowledge such a rule, we should be at a loss to know why, in principle, he preferred life to death.

There is thus at least a possibility, to put it at its lowest, that our four criteria would meet his case. For they are all concerned with the maximisation of desire and of satisfaction. Besides this, of course, he needs an ego which is not only in good communication with his desires but in good communication with the outside world: we do not need to be told that the satisfaction of our desires depends on our understanding of the outside world and the people in it; and of course in practice he will have to compromise. But at least he will now know *what* he is compromising: we shall have given him some sort of ideal.

2 The second reason for adopting such criteria is at once simpler and more compelling. The questioner accepts his own uncertainty about what to be: and the only general guiding principle we can unhesitatingly offer him is a principle designed to put him in the best position for choice. It follows that he should, ideally, *try himself out* as an entity with varying desires, experiencing them as fully as possible: and it is here that our first criterion, the necessity of a well-developed ego which can inspect and order the desires, is of the greatest importance. Briefly, the best position in which to decide what to be is only achieved by (a) being able to incorporate an infinite variety of ends and desires, and (b) having an ego which preserves ideal communication within the self. It is plain that this represents an ideal situation, a limiting case, which is never reached: and can never be reached, because the possibilities of extending human nature and developing the human ego are infinite.

The point here is analogous to what has often been said about the importance of imagination and perceptivity in moral problems, but it is not identical. For before we can deploy such imaginative insight into other people and their situations, we have to be able to use it on ourselves. Insight into others is achieved by our being able to recognise ourselves or parts of ourselves in them: hence we have first to recognise ourselves. In this respect also how we see ourselves lies behind our morality in relation to others.

These criteria, and the principles which they suggest, find a Plato-like echo in criteria which we commonly hold to apply to society. We are familiar with the views that a society should be (1) so organised that the communication is good between rulers and ruled, and between different parts of the society, (2) not apathetic or lifeless, but rather intense and vital, (3) harmonious, integrated, well ordered, and (4) varied, not narrow, 'multivalent'. Indeed one might call this a liberal view of society, since it is essentially similar to liberal views of morality conceived in terms of the mutual satisfaction of desires or interests. But such an outlook can only be justified by connecting it with an answer to 'What shall I be?' which is at once sufficiently general and sufficiently compelling.

We can now also perceive, at least dimly, how it is that worries about gaining more freedom are connected with worries about being more rational, and perhaps in the end turn out to be the same worry. By our criteria, being more free and being more rational both necessitate being more of a person, accepting and controlling a greater range of desires. Moreover, since we can only justify our own ideals and rules by reference to these criteria, which are no more than the criteria of sanity pushed to an extreme, it seems that our business as people is primarily to make every effort to live up to them in so far as we understand them, and our business as thinkers to make them more understandable. This would certainly alter our attitude to morality, and perhaps to moral philosophy also.

This reminds us of a very old thesis: the thesis that some people—those whom philosophers have variously described as wise, sensible, right-thinking, or just 'good'—are in fact in a better position to frame moral principles than others. Their wisdom consists, not merely in those comparatively superficial qualities which we call 'reasonableness', but in their power to penetrate the depths of the human psyche and attain a more profound awareness of what the basic human desires actually are. Whatever techniques may help us to do this also help to reinforce the rather shaky analogy made by the ancient Greeks between morality and medicine. The shakiness of this analogy has often been thought of as primarily due to an error of logic: a failure to notice that we only accept doctors as experts because we already share certian values in regard to the state of our bodies. But it is *logically* possible to prefer what we call ill health to what we call health: though in practice few people do. So too in matters of morality it is not logically contradictory to frame what rules we choose: though here, because we appear to have different ends, one person frames rules very different from another. But it is not clear that we really do have different ends: or rather (if we take 'end' to mean 'conscious objective') that we really do have basically dissimilar desires. The analogy is weak not because you cannot justify ultimate moral values in the same way as you can justify the lower-order rules for health which depend on pre-existent criteria, but because we do not know as much about psychology as we do about medicine.

The expertise of a moral expert is open to abuse precisely to the degree to which we are psychologically ignorant. If somebody tries to persuade me that I do not 'really want' something which I say I want and (consciously) do want, the chances are that he is trying to bully me: he may even use this phrase as a disguise for his own moral judgements. On the other hand, there are plenty of cases when we can use the phrase significantly. We frequently say of a child that he does not 'really want' something, although he thinks he does: moreover, we often consider our view justified by subsequent events, such as the child's pronouncing itself satisfied or simply appearing satisfied. Further, and more importantly, when we say of things in our own past history: 'I didn't really want that: I only thought I did', we are not just saying that our wants have changed. The assertion of the lover who says, 'It was you I wanted all the time', though paradoxical, is not nonsense. It bears witness to the *recognition* of wants or desires which were, in a quite non-technical sense, unconscious.

It may be thought utopian or wildly optimistic to assume that the basic desires of men are sufficiently similar to give them all the same justification for adopting the same moral rules. But few psychologists would maintain that human beings are born with radically different desires: still less that they are born with moral opinions, whether similar to each other or different. Differences result from the different case-histories of similar desires, during which certain desires become repressed or distorted, and the rational self, as yet too weak to face squarely the conflict between its own desires and the harsh external world, loses touch with them to a greater or lesser extent. This is not a difference in human nature, but in the histories of various human beings; and it is in principle possible for a human being to retrace his history and thereby improve the system of communication within his own personality. The efficiency of this system is our chief criterion for rationality.

It would be tedious, and perhaps prejudicial, to phrase this point in the technical terms of psychoanalysis. But whether the technique of psychoanalysis is all that it is made out to be or not, it gives us at least a conceivable method of settling moral differences along the lines I have suggested. For the technique is supposed to be a method of making the individual more aware of his own desires, strengthening his ego so that he can accept himself more fully for what he is and hence choose more rationally, rather than a method of indoctrinating him with a different set of values or in any direct way changing his moral opinions. The rational person would be the person whose values would remain the same even after the most exhaustive analysis: the irrational person would come to see that his moral views were based on distortions of desires which he had not fully faced.

Most moral thinkers in the past, and not a few in the present, assume that the only rational justification for a moral opinion must, so to speak, extend outwards and upwards, away from the choosing self. I believe that X is wrong: I justify this in terms of a rule: this in turn is justified in terms of a higher rule, and so on: until perhaps I find myself building a watertight system of metaphysical morality, a giant framework of absolute and externalised rules, or even a political utopia in which all my desires, or what I believe to be my desires, find full expression. But there is a kind of rational justification which moves in a different direction, inwards and downwards into the human psyche: and it is to this that we have to turn, retracing our steps down the pyramid of moral criteria that we have (often fantastically) erected, back to the self. This process has its own methods and its own logic: and it is primarily by the classification of these, in my view, that the moral philosopher can be useful. Here I have space only to point to a vast unexplored area.

This view of the matter also accounts for the fact that the moral arguments and discussions which are profitable to us are not always those which pay the closest attention to rules and logic. Profitable conversations are those in which we come to see ourselves, and hence other people, in a different light: in which we somehow come to recognise something that had hitherto been hidden from us. Moral arguments have often been compared to lawsuits, in which advocates 'present the facts' in a way which is compelling to any 'reasonable man', though not with the compulsion of logical demonstration. An apter comparison might be with the arguments, if we can call them such, presented by the literary critic: for this does more justice to the complexity of the situation, which the phrase 'present the facts' in the former comparison fatally disguises. It is not merely the *external* facts which a good moral counsellor presents: what he does is to show us ourselves to ourselves—to show us, if we must speak of 'facts', the *internal* facts. So too the literary critic does not deal only, or even chiefly, with the hard facts about a poem: indeed, so far as he is concerned with empirical data, such as its date, authorship, legibility, and so on, he is only functioning as one sort of literary critic, and perhaps a rather unimportant sort, whose business is really more historical than literary. He is really attempting to work on the sensibilities and feelings of the reader, to evoke a recognition and a response, to clear the reader's mind and allow him to see the literary work for what it is, free from bewitchment or prejudice.

There is, I believe, a whole range of operations, not all of which could reasonably be called arguments, which human beings use in approaching morality. Some of these, such as hypnosis and brain-washing, are indoctrinatory: and these methods do not result in an increase of rational awareness. Others are not: and they might vary from direct and timely action to a strictly formal argument. For example, suppose I am trying to persuade you to contribute to famine relief, or to a fund for the cure of leprosy. I might actually show you a starving child or a leper: or I might take you to a film in which starvation or leprosy was a central theme: or I might tell you a story, perhaps in the form of a fictitious parable (like the Good Samaritan): or I might use various verbal or practical devices, like squibs, to shock you out of your present attitude of complacency: or I might try to make you aware in discussion of the causes of your present attitude—perhaps you have not learned to identify sufficiently with other people, so that your complacency reflects a general incapacity to love, or perhaps you are unconsciously scared of identifying with them, in case it makes you feel intolerably insecure, so that your complacency is merely a self-protective mask. All these methods, and many more are open to me besides those (which alone we are accustomed to describe as the methods of 'reason') whereby I would try to persuade you of the inconsistency of your refusal to contribute: but they are rational methods, and much more likely to bear fruit.

In fact the picture is even wider than this. Any and every kind of reasoning may be demanded of us as moral beings: there is no single set of contexts which we can describe as 'moral reasoning' or 'the methods of morality'. Thus a moral error may result not only, as I have been emphasising, from lack of awareness or imagination, but more simply from a failure to attend to the laws of logic or to the hard empirical facts. A man may contradict himself, knowingly or without noticing, and he may refuse or fail to observe the direct empirical consequences of his action. Such a person may, if he is very obstinate or very mentally disturbed, refuse to play the same reason-games as his fellows. He may say 'I don't care about the facts': or even 'I don't care if I do contradict myself'. Such a man would be a super-fanatic: like Hare's moral fanatics, only worse. I suspect that super-fanatics, like fanatics, are far more common than most of us suppose: and it is not wholly irrelevant to consider how we should deal with them.

After what we have already said, the answer to this will not be surprising. We have to show the super-fanatic that his attitude is self-defeating: that it does not get him what he wants. If he says 'Why should I obey the law of non-contradiction?' we reply 'This law is not a wicked imposition on the part of philosophers, and by all means break it if you like: only, you will find it very difficult to talk or even to think. For if you allow yourself to say "so-and-so" in one breath, and "not so-and-so" in the next breath, you will find that you haven't said anything at all, you have just uttered noises. Now, surely you find talking and thinking useful for getting what you want: so if you accept the value of talking and thinking, you thereby accept the laws of logic, of which this law is one.' Similarly if he says: 'Why should I attend to the facts?' we can reply: 'Because you know quite well that it's only by attending to the facts that you can make successful predictions about what will happen if you do this or that: you can save yourself disappointment, gain your objective more easily, and so forth—it's in your own interest to attend to the facts.'

In this way it can be seen how all the language-games we create and play, and in terms of which the truth or acceptability of statements are judged, depend ultimately upon human purposes. They are means by which we attempt to gain more control over the world and over ourselves, so that we can gain our ends. Sometimes, as in the case of the natural sciences, one particular game produces remarkably good results in a comparatively short time. Sometimes we cannot see exactly what *sort* of human ends a particular game is supposed to serve, and hence cannot judge whether it is worth playing or what rules to play it by. This is, I think, still true of the kind of talk that we come across in Marx and Freud, and certainly true of religious talk.

It is tempting here to draw a rough distinction between two general classes of games: first, those which directly enable us to predict what will happen in the outside world—that is, in effect, the sciences; and second, those whose function is to improve our own ability as observers and actors in the world. Thus it may be that the prime importance of the work of Marx and Freud is not scientific (though they may have so conceived it), but to render our minds more flexible, to free them from having to look at social and individual behaviour in certain fixed ways, and to enable us to look at them in a more objective spirit—a spirit which has no room for prejudice, traditionalism, or a barely concealed belief in magic. The work of philosophy falls into this general class: so too may the work of religion, and activities such as literature, literary criticism and the arts in general. The criteria for success in these activities, however, are far from clear: and they will remain so until we are clearer about what kinds of games are really in accord with human purposes, and what kinds only seem to be.

Although it would not be sufficiently germane to the subject to pursue this particular point, the importance of this kind of rational methodology as a whole is far from irrelevant. This is not only because the principles of equality, like other principles, must be justified by reference to a rationally defensible ideal. It is also because we shall be inclined to measure political and other ideals, not only by whether they *flow from* an increased awareness of human nature, but also by whether they *contribute to* such awareness. To put it briefly, if there is anything in the notion of treating people as equals which is ideally justifiable, this is likely to be so not only because that is what rational people would desire, but also because that is what would *make people rational*. It is primarily for this reason that I have dealt at some length with the question of rational justification as a whole.

2

The Need for
Equality

What I shall maintain in this section may be more easily
grasped with the aid of a preview. Briefly, I shall claim that
equality is the *formal* aspect of a liberal ideal which the
points made in the last section show to be necessary for all
rational people. 'Treating people as equals' is, as it were, the
description of the skeleton of a particular way of life, whose
flesh is made up of the content of other concepts, in particular those of fraternity, communication, and love. One
might describe equality as a logical prerequisite for these
ideals, as well as for the less substantial concepts of liberty,
democracy, justice, and others that form part of the stock-
in-trade of liberalism.

The best way to start is to see how these liberal concepts,
which we saw to be incoherent in themselves, gain substance
when related to a particular ideal. What the liberal really
has to offer is a particular kind of relationship between human
beings, *a particular form of communication*. Certain kinds
of human contact, in his view, are ideally to be desired—
roughly, those kinds in which I treat you as an equal; do not
use force, threats or any kind of pressure on you; communicate with you rather than oppress you; educate you
rather than indoctrinate you; behave towards you as to a
brother rather than as to a superior or inferior. If this ideal
is to be defended, it has to be shown to satisfy human ends.
But the liberal does not have to maintain that it corresponds
to the existing conscious desires or intentions of all men
as they now are: indeed, this is plainly false, since many
people prefer master-slave relationships to relationships of
equality. They prefer a context of command and obedience,

of pressure and counter-pressure, to a context of communication. All he has to show is that it is ultimately irrational to prefer such relationships and contexts, though we have to remember that he has to show it to be irrational, not only for men as they are, but for any conscious and animate creature.

The notion that what liberals and egalitarians really have to sell is a particular kind of communication—a way of doing business, so to speak—also sheds some new light on the old liberal problem of conflicting ends. Thus Isaiah Berlin writes: '. . . the belief that some single formula can in principle be found whereby all the diverse ends of men can be harmoniously realised is demonstrably false. If, as I believe, the ends of men are many, and not all of them are in principle compatible with each other, then the possibility of conflict—and of tragedy—can never wholly be eliminated from human life, either personal or social.'[1] But this can only be maintained if we take our conscious wants and intentions as ultimately authoritative: and if that were so, we could not engage in rational ethics at all. For rational ethics presuppose that we can employ some rational *method to change* our conscious wants and intentions for the better: or, to put it another way, that we can come to *recognise* that what we took to be our ends were not our 'real' ends. What the liberal has to sell is a method of change, a milieu in which recognition can take place.

Thus it may be seen that the liberal ideal operates at two levels, and has two distinct kinds of justification. First, the liberal maintains that a particular context of communication is good as a means: that it is the best method of enabling people to discover what their real ends are, and hence to satisfy them. Secondly, he maintains that, once people have become properly aware of this context and can use it to the full, they will find their real ends precisely in perfecting and using it. One of the tasks of the political philosopher is to describe this context in formal terms: if he does not succeed in doing this, liberalism is bound to seem no more than a vague plea for tolerance and moderation, backed by a number of fashionable but vacuous concepts. But once we have seen this, it becomes plain that the kind of rules and

1. I. Berlin, *Two Concepts of Liberty* (O.U.P.), p. 54.

principles which would form such a description are not those which we are accustomed to consider under the category of 'politics'. They seem more closely connected with the subject-matter of sociology and psychology: and it is, in fact, on a mixture of psychological fact and ordinary logic that the liberal has to rest his case.

Some examples may make this clearer. There are two reasons why, if two nations have conflicting desires, we think it better for their leaders to discuss the situation round a table than for the nations to go to war. First, the context of discussion is a more efficient milieu than the context of war for enabling both sides to change their desires in a rational direction. If the context is properly used, each party will be able to understand the nature of his own and the other's desires, by relating them in conversation to other people. He will need to be able to identify emotionally with the other party, to communicate with him as a person: and there is then hope of reaching some agreement. Secondly, we feel that this context represents, in microcosm, the way in which the two nations should be living together. It is not only a means to an end: it is an attempt to create the fulfilment of that end in miniature. This is *why* the context gives hope of agreement: we feel that, once the two parties really understand and identify with each other, they will both come to see that what they really want, more than anything else, is precisely to co-exist in this harmonious state of understanding and identification.

The same two reasons apply when we ask why a husband and wife should use some forms of communication, such as words and caresses, rather than others, such as insults or blows. Not only is the former a more efficient method of settling differences: it is also a better method of living, an end in itself. In such a case one might say, somewhat poetically, that the purpose of rational communication is simply to improve itself: to maximise satisfaction to the degree experienced by two people deeply in love. Hence the kind of rules and principles which we have to describe will be psychological or educational in nature: they will be, in effect, rules for loving—or, if 'love' is thought to take us too far away from politics, for fraternity.

The question now arises why fraternity should claim any

more logical or rational backing than any other ideal, such as the ideals of the superman or the slave. It might be thought sufficient to say that the methods mentioned in the last section, whereby we increase our awareness and understanding of our own desires, do in fact result in our coming to recognise fraternity as a greater means of satisfaction than say, sadism or masochism. This I believe to be true: but I think we can say a little more.

First, to take human beings as they in fact are, it is inevitable that a man should define his own identity, acquire his own desires, and gain control of the means of satisfying them by relating himself to other people and to the outside world in general. Without this, which is no more than the normal process of growing up, he would hardly be human. Hence he is bound, as it were, to commit himself to things and people in the world: he has, at the least, to acknowledge their existence, and accept them for what they are—otherwise he will fail to understand them, and hence fail to relate to them and control them. A child who did not, at some point and to some degree, learn to use criteria of similarity which defined for him the concept of *another person*, with a will like his own, would not himself grow up into a person. His humanity, and certainly his sanity, would depend on his ability to relate to other people and communicate with them.

But this point can be generalised. We could assume the existence of animate creatures who did not relate or communicate, who were wholly cut off from their fellows (though they could not have anything we could call a society, and would be nothing like any human beings we know of, except perhaps for certain types of advanced psychotic). But these entities would plainly not be gaining as much satisfaction as they could gain, since it is always possible to increase satisfaction by relating in some way to the external world. Even if we imagine them in separate boxes, being looked after by servo-mechanisms which instantly satisfy their every want, they could still not rationally be content: for it would always be possible for them to create and satisfy new wants, found in the world outside, or to satisfy their existing wants more intensely by improving their servo-mechanisms. What this somewhat futuristic example shows is that some degree of commitment to the external world is logically necessary for any animate creature : perhaps an obvious truth, but an important one.

But, secondly, the nature of the commitment is just as important. If a man wants to gain satisfaction from the external world, the objects and entities in that world must be (at least potentially) a source of pleasure for him. Moreover—and this cuts out the sadist—they must be a source of pleasure for what they are in themselves, and not for any pleasure he can gain in diminishing, destroying or distorting them. For sadists, and in general those who hate rather than love, do not in reality accept the world as a source of satisfaction. They are against it : they wish it were otherwise, or wish to destroy it altogether. This is not, of course, to say that we ought in practice always to adjust ourselves to the world rather than vice versa. To do so might be in many cases impossible, and in many cases undesirable, since we might thereby fail to obtain as much satisfaction as we could. But it remains true in principle that the more the world is, so to speak, a *good thing* for us rather than a thing to be attacked or destroyed—the more we say 'Yes' to it rather than snarling at it—then the more satisfaction we are likely to have.

The general logic of this point also can be clarified, if we consider the case of suicide. Some suicides are, of course, rational : if I am in the hands of torturers and likely to remain there, life is no longer worth living, because the dissatisfaction outweighs the satisfaction. But if I were the sort of person who could be tortured and still gain enough satisfaction to make life worth living—perhaps I could switch on a masochistic disposition, or contemplate the Absolute and so forget the pain—it would be irrational to kill myself. If I can get a balance of satisfaction, then there is always a point of life. This is a logical truth : answers to questions of the form 'What is the point of . . .?' must always be given in terms of human satisfaction : a statement like 'There's no point in getting satisfaction' would have no clear sense. That is why we condemn suicide as irrational, when the person could (as in the hands of torturers I cannot) quite possibly find some satisfaction in his life, even if it seems to hold none at present : and it may also be why those who commit suicide, whose situation in life is often quite enviable from any other viewpoint but the purely psychological, frequently seem to be striving for some 'point' or 'meaning' to life which they insist should be beyond the whole realm and apparatus of human satisfaction, and hence is logically impossible.

The suicide is only the extreme case of those who deny life, and who wish to destroy or suppress rather than create and enlarge. The egalitarian on the other hand will try to make other creatures as equal with himself as he can, because this will extend and improve his own relationships. In some cases, as with human infants, he can succeed in this task to the full, by making people out of creatures that in infancy more closely resemble animals: and even with *bona fide* animals he will endeavour to communicate and educate so far as he can. This is because he wants *friends*: and he can get the most out of friends if they can be treated as equals. It is in this sense that equality acts as the formal framework of fraternity.

It is hence not accidental that the French Revolutionaries placed 'fraternity' alongside 'equality': for it should now be fairly plain why a belief in intrinsic equality is rational. As we saw at the end of Part Two there is an important gap between simply *noting the metaphysical or logical fact* that all men are equal, and *determining to treat people as equals*. This gap is filled by the necessity of fraternity: more precisely, by the impossibility of being fraternal unless one is prepared to identify with the other person. To identify, to put yourself in his shoes, is essentially to regard him as a being like yourself, whose aims and purposes are as valid as your own. This is the starting-point, not only for the concepts of liberalism, but for any rational morality. Once you make this move, the abstract considerations advanced earlier in this book immediately begin to carry weight. If you look on your neighbour in this light, you have to grant him equal scope and equal powers with yourself: you consider his criteria, whether of language or of value, to be on a par with your own.

The general features of egalitarian thought, as we have noted them in earlier chapters, should now fall into place behind the ideal of intrinsic equality. In Part One[1] we

1. See pp. 40–56.

endeavoured to tackle the notions of natural and artificial similarity. We found that, although the egalitarian could make various important practical distinctions, these distinctions seemed in the last resort abitrary, in that they depended ultimately on human choices and the criteria of human language. To this we can now add, first, that we cannot rationally impose choices and criteria upon others: and secondly, that we can test the rationality of our choices and criteria by the ideal of good communication. In this context the ability to gain greater control and understanding of our environment by making better predictions plays a large part: and this is plainly necessary for better communication, as well as for the more obvious human ends which are the preconditions of communication—such as obtaining food and avoiding death.

But it would be a mistake to suppose that the only, or even the primary, purpose of language is descriptive, as if in talking and writing we were only concerned with activities like naming, measuring, or predicting. On this view we might be tempted to suppose it logically open for anyone to adopt whatever linguistic criteria he liked, just as (we might think) he can adopt whatever moral criteria and make whatever choices he likes. But in fact we do not use language only as a tool for mastering and exploiting the outside world for our own ends: we use it as a psychological link between man and man, and must remember not just its descriptive functions but also such activities as reassuring, expressing emotion, making love, conducting common rituals, and so on. This bears some witness to our recognition of language as serving the common end of communication, so that we must proceed as members of a group of equals: I cannot, by the very nature of language itself, frame criteria in virtue of which I regard people as if they were no more than objects. This 'group of equals' is coextensive with all rational creatures. Even the most alien monster from outer space, if he were a conscious and intelligent being, would have learnt his language from other monsters: and he would be bound to make distinctions, in that language, between rational and non-rational entities. If he treated human beings as ants, he would be guilty of inconsistency by his own criteria.

The relevance of the 'accidental' equalities among men and

their potentiality as contributors, which we noticed in Part Two, and of egalitarian thought that we noted when considering equality as a political principle in Part One, also becomes more intelligible. By learning to identify, we learn to see another person as he sees himself: and he sees himself primarily as a willing, choosing creature, with certain central characteristics (as perhaps his intelligence, and some of his desires), and certain characteristics which he regards, not as part of himself, but as things thrust upon him by fate (as perhaps his wealth, birth, looks or social position). Consequently we are bound to set up those social rules which are framed in terms of his will and his central characteristics, to play those games in which these things, and not the things thrust upon him by fate, count for most and are mostly rewarded.

Thus the reason why it is a move towards greater equality that intelligence and hard work, rather than wealth, should be rewarded by university entrance, or some other educational privilege, is ultimately that this particular arrangement does more justice to the way in which people see themselves. We saw in Part One how a great deal turns on our picture of the person who plays these social games, on how we use the word 'he' in sentences like 'He deserves a reward', 'He has more opportunity', and so on. It is characteristic of non-egalitarian rules that 'he' is used *according to the speaker's own criteria of personality*, and not according to the criteria of the person he is talking about. But to do this is to ignore the importance of intrinsic equality as an operative principle, because it ignores the importance of identification. The whole trend of the attempt to obtain some absolute justice or 'fair play' is evidence of the egalitarian desire to make people's wills count. We can also see how it was that the egalitarian inevitably finds himself driven away from the idea of social competition and towards the idea of co-operation. For the only context in which he can be sure of everybody's will counting equally is a context of co-operation or communication, where we strive for a common end. Our rules are then self-imposed, and it is no longer the case that one set of rules suits one man, and another another man: since our ends are agreed, we simply have to find the most efficient rules to follow in order to fulfil them.

It may seem that disagreement about which are the most efficient rules to follow for fulfilling a common end is likely to be as bad as disagreement about ends: or even that it amounts to disagreement about ends in a new form. But this is not so. We have not, indeed, agreed about a specific end, in the sense that we could draw a detailed blue-print of an ideal individual or an ideal state. This kind of agreement would certainly be irrational, and could only be temporary: for new forms of life and new possibilities of communication and development always arise. But we should have agreed about the *general description* of the common end, in terms which would not be wholly devoid of factual content (we should not merely have paraphrased 'the ideal life' by another word, such as 'happiness'); and also we should have agreed about a general method for finding out how to fill in the details and make new advances. We should have seen that other descriptions and other methods were, at least in part, either otiose, or inadequate, or logically mistaken. It would not be too much to say that once we have seen that the common end for all rational creatures consists in fraternal communication, our disagreements will be reduced to disagreements about the efficiency of various techniques of communication. Nobody would pretend that it would be easy to overcome such disagreements, but it would be an immense gain even to have reduced the difficulty to such proportions. To put it crudely, we should then at least be studying the right subject: we should be able to direct our attention to those experts who analyse and compare the respective efficiency of different contexts and methods of communication.

Here the context of psychoanalysis stands as a model case, not because of any truth or falsity in the claims of psychoanalytic theory, but because it is at least intended to be a context designed specifically for the improvement of the ability to communicate and the ability to love. There is an important sense in which the patient, even though he is mentally ill, is treated as an equal: his desires and the expression of his desires are not crushed: he is not subject to force, threats, emotional pressure or even advice on the part of the analyst: he is not made to feel guilty, wicked, ashamed, or frightened. He is encouraged to be himself and to become

F

aware of himself. He is educated, but not indoctrinated.

The intentions of such a technique (I claim nothing about the practice of it) make it into a model case, beside which all other relationships which are not already based on love and the fulfilment of mutual need appear as at best clumsy. If we are already working for a common end, as when we are playing in an orchestra together, or actually engaged in harmonious communication, as when we make love or swap jokes, then the principle of equality is already satisfied. But when there is some kind of conflict, either in politics or in personal relationships, all our techniques fall short of the egalitarian principle. Whether we use wars, propaganda, anger, frowns, or sulky silences we invariably employ some kind of pressure. Part of the reason for this deficiency is no doubt that we simply do not know of other and better techniques. But it is mostly because we do not realise the desirability of such techniques. We positively prefer to treat the other person as an enemy, or as a superior, or as an inferior: at any rate, not as an equal. Equality-relationships are very hard to sustain, and demand a high degree of psychological maturity. It is not to be wondered at if we often fail to sustain them: but usually we do not even try.

The sensible egalitarian will, of course, recognise that his ideal is not even understood by the majority of people, and that even if they were to understand it they would lack the psychic strength to actualise it. He will observe that in many countries people prefer to regard themselves as the inferior of some ruler or dictator who acts as some kind of father-figure to them, and that in non-political contexts there are a vast majority who prefer to command or be commanded, rather than to work things out with their equals. Nearly everybody (though they might deny it) finds such a context more reassuring and less frightening. In a very real sense it is *restful* to be in the army, where you have simply to give and take orders, or to be fighting a war where there is a boss (Churchill) and an enemy (Hitler): in both cases everything is clear-cut, your duties and obligations are fixed and certain. You know where you are. It is like being a child again, going back to a time of life when you are told what to do, and can be certain of support: when there are 'good' men and 'bad' men, and you know beyond a doubt what you are supposed to love and what to hate.

Realising this, the egalitarian will not be so foolish as to expect very many people to be able to make anything like full use of rational contexts of communication. He will defend himself against his irrational enemies, since although he regards them as equals he does not have to regard them as superiors. Apart from self-defence, his treatment of them will always be such as to educate them to communicate. He will use only such methods as enlarge their personalities rather than diminish them: methods which increase their self-awareness and hence the rational scope of their wills. He does this, not as a technique to gain his own particular liberal ends, but as a technique to help them gain their own ends. Freedom of communication is not a weapon which the liberals use in advancing their own ideal, but part of that ideal itself.

It is not surprising that egalitarians have, in general, been opposed to acceptance of traditional authority, preferring to place what sometimes seems a rather naive trust in human nature. For the acceptance of any authority, other than the authority of the facts or of those who are expert in the facts, rightly seems to him a sign of immaturity, a denial of that equal and independent status which is every man's right. His naivety about human nature may be forgiven him when we remember that the first clear (though sometimes fitful) light was only shed on the unconscious mind some fifty years ago, and that what we may call the *density* and opaqueness of human nature and human desires are still not properly appreciated. In the past, most religious, moral and political authorities have represented themselves as if they were factual experts: as if they simply gave out factual truths about how men ought to behave. The realisation (not only by analytic philosophers) that these factual truths cannot be given out quite so simply in fields of discourse which are primarily concerned with a choice of values has left a gap, indeed an intense feeling of disappointment. Those modern works of literature and philosophy which we may describe under the general title of 'existentialist' do not fill this gap: indeed, they are intended to demonstrate it and increase our awareness of it. We can only fill it by accepting (if we must have authorities) those who are authorities not of facts but of methods: those who impart not truths but skills. Communicating, doing morality, playing politics, understanding ourselves and other people—these are plainly more like learning to talk or to swim than they are like learning mathematics or Latin grammar.

Since the egalitarian will not be so naive as to expect that his ideal of equality-relationships can be achieved at one blow, he will not be doctrinaire about his choice of political and social contexts. Recognising that this choice must be governed by psychological fact rather than political catch-phrases, he will recommend those contexts which individuals can best tolerate and learn from. Thus, questions about authority-figures in the state, such as whether we ought to have a monarch or a president, whom people will look up to, or about such figures in more obviously educational contexts, such as how strongly the headmaster of a school should allow his own personality to operate, are not to be answered by a naive traditionalism or an equally naive egalitarianism. They need to be settled solely by regard to the psychological facts about the average Englishman or American, and the average adolescent. It is not difficult to see that human beings only make progress towards equality-relationships—only learn to grow up, we might say—by a series of local identifications which begin with their parents, move on perhaps to a schoolmaster, a gang leader or some other quasi-hero, and only too often end up with a king, a dictator, a millionaire, or a film star. Even those who con-sciously seek, or at least purport to seek, equality-relation-ships with their fellow-men find it easier if they are able to identify with some one figure, usually superhuman, who in-carnates this ideal—Christ, Buddha, Marx, or even Freud.

How much we can expect people to transmute these local identifications into a belief in the intrinsic equality of all men is, of course, too large and too vague a question to be answered in detail here. But with regard to the more sophis-ticated peoples of the world—and I refer primarily to those countries who have a high standard of living and some tradition of liberalism—there seems to be an excess of vague idealism and a dearth of effective techniques. Many of us are anxious about our own incapacity to love, and work off our guilt by the (in themselves) admirable devices of helping the underprivileged, giving aid to under-developed countries, protesting against the lack of freedom in certain parts of the world, supporting movements for pacifism and intentional amity, and so forth. When divorce, delinquency, and neurosis (to say nothing of other evidence) so evidently demonstrate us to be incapable of loving our wives, our children, or even ourselves, such behaviour seems a little suspect. Learning to love is hard work, and charity begins at home.

Our behaviour in political and social contexts in fact suggests that we are usually more concerned with *equity* than with equality. We want our rights, or what we conceive to be our rights: we do not want partnership. Thus it is not at all clear that strikers, or trade unionists in general, are activated by a desire to achieve equality or partnership with the management: the notion of co-operative ownership (as distinct from a vague left-wing desire for nationalisation) does not play a large part in their motives. Strikers want shorter hours and better pay: more status, and perhaps more power: but not an equality-relationship. Feminist agitators in general, and the British suffragettes in particular, are more plausibly represented as demanding justice than as demanding partnership: and though it is no doubt preferable that a marriage should consist of two equally armed camps rather than one armed and one helpless, it is a long way from the kind of equality-relationship we have been discussing. Nor does the general political scene differ from these particular examples: 'we' make very little effort, and perhaps have very little desire, to run our own political lives in partnership with our fellows, as long as 'they'—and this may mean anything from the Prime Minister to the income-tax collector—treat us well, give us a reasonable standard of living, and do not too overtly interfere with our individual liberty.

Once the egalitarian reformist has realised that his values are to be cashed out in terms of techniques of communication he will be able to see his way through an impasse which has held up many liberal thinkers. In all social and human contexts, and not least in politics, there is always a choice between confirming a traditional authority and rebelling against it. This may be represented, depending on the context, as a choice between conservatism and radicalism, between orthodox and subversive beliefs, between the super-ego and the id, between political conformism or political agitation, or between the establishment and the underprivileged. Very often it can be represented as a choice between contentment and progress, acceptance and struggle, or integration and expansion. For most of our techniques either confirm us in quietism, which may keep us happy but will not lead to progress, or else disturb and unsettle us, which may result in greater awareness and a change for the better but will threaten our security and integration. These terms may seem vague. What I have in mind is a set of specific questions, such as 'Should we start a revolution, or hope for more peaceful change?', 'How far shall I permit or encourage this boy to question the morality his parents have taught him?', 'Shall we upset the religious beliefs of this primitive tribe, which are plainly false but which form the framework of their society?': and in general the question 'Shall we give people a good shake-up, or reassure them?'

In practice our answers to such questions have been dictated by the notions of 'moderation', 'not going too far (or too fast)', 'a reasonable compromise', and so forth. These notions are usually accepted by tradition; and conflicts arise where one tradition clashes with another. Thus one particular speed in handing over colonies for self-government may seem reasonable to the British Colonial Office, and another quite different speed to the inhabitants of the colonies. We are here arguing, or ought to be arguing, about the respective merits of different contexts of learning: and the matter could in principle be settled if the psychological facts were agreed by both sides. But the criterion for such a context needs clarification: for compromise is not here a logical necessity. We are not logically compelled to put up with a certain amount of disintegration for the sake of change, or with a certain amount of ignorance and stupidity for the sake of peace and quiet. As the model case of psychoanalysis shows, it is possible for a context both to strengthen and to enlarge the personality at the same time. The antitheses set out above are forced on us by practical incompetence not by the nature of the case. It has indeed often been stressed by liberals that adaptability and awareness are sources of strength as well as of progress. But all depends on the awareness coming in the right context. A good adviser, moralist politician, or educationalist should be able to increase both the integration and the freedom of those with whom he deals. If he does not, no solid ground has been gained.

This is a direct consequence of an equality-relationship. For a mistake on either side, whether by smothering a man's consciousness in an attempt to keep him on an even keel, or by disintegrating it in an attempt to make him more aware, is always evidence that we have failed to treat him as an equal. In the first instance we have allowed his will to atrophy: in the second we have broken it: in neither have we enlarged him as a person. Such cases always imply either technical incompetence, or our own inability to sustain a relationship of equality. If we can manage such a relationship, then we have no need to worry about 'going too far or too fast'; in this sense there cannot be too much communication or too much equality.

Some light is also shed on the problem of expertise in political and social contexts. If we conceive of politics, education and morality as fields in which, to put it briefly, it is rational that those who know should dictate to those who do not, then the notion of intrinsic equality is almost worthless. Not wholly worthless: for since the values of each individual are as valid as those of any other, the individual must *freely* place himself in the hands of these experts—those who balance budgets, decide on a wages policy, dictate foreign affairs, tell us how to bring up our children, ordain our sex lives, and so on. But it is conceivable, with the advance of sociology and psychology, that the area in which one man's opinion is as good as another's may shrink to an infinitesimal size. This would be worrying, if it did not rest on a misconception which divided these fields of discourse without remainder into two things: science and expertise on the one hand, and individual choice on the other. It is only by virtue of this misconception that we can plausibly represent the individual's life as increasingly passive. The man chooses his end—good health, a happy marriage, a high standard of living: and then some expert tells him how to get it. There seems no room for individual effort: like a child, one simply says what one wants and is given it.

A state of good communication, however, is in principle

not something which you can be *given*. It is something which you yourself have to create and participate in: otherwise it would not be a relationship of equality, but of inferiority. There is of course a sense in which the psycho-analyst or the wise parent acts as superior to the patient or the child: but there is also a clear sense in which they act as equals, and build a joint relationship. You may learn the skills of life, if we may call them so, from experts: but you cannot get experts to deploy them for you, for your life precisely *is* the deploying of these skills. An expert musician may teach you to play the violin better, but if you want to play the violin at all you cannot allow him to play it *for* you all the time.

Finally, it is perhaps worth pointing out that the strength of the egalitarian case which I have tried to build up does not entitle the egalitarian to impose his views on others, however irrational (by the terms of this case) they may be. He may, of course, appear to impose on others in order to obtain the preconditions for communication: among these preconditions, obviously, are things like life, health, enough food, freedom from pain, and so forth. Thus he will push a man out of the path of an oncoming car, if there is no time to argue with him. But he will only do such things if justified by the consciously held ends of the individual concerned: if the man genuinely desires to kill himself, he will let him. He may sometimes have to guess at what the conscious ends of a person actually are: and very often it will not be clear what they are, even if the person himself tries to give an account of them. (This is often the case with children or very backward people.) But he will not feel entitled to override them *simply* because they are young, or stupid, or neurotic, or suicidal. For they are still his equals.

PART FIVE

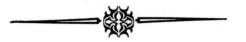

EQUALITY
IN PRACTICE

I want now to illustrate some of the points already made by applying them to practical contexts. Since the proper practical application of any concept depends very largely on empirical facts, I cannot offer more than a few sketches which will inevitably lack substance, but from which we may at least be able to see how our findings could in principle be applied—how they would bear on the empirical situation, whatever it may be. The reader will appreciate that these topics properly require far more detailed treatment: and I must apologise in advance both to those who would have preferred a fuller account and to those who would have preferred nothing at all.

The concept of equality may be deployed in three types of practical context. First, there is the context in which some people have a mandate to make up rules for others— parents for children, governments for their citizens, and so on. Secondly, there is the context in which, by tradition or custom, some people are regarded as superior in class or status to others, as aristocrats are often taken to be superior to commoners. Thirdly, there is the context in which people of equal status make up rules for themselves, as in marriage, friendships, and many informal associations. I shall choose one example from each context.

I

The Power Élite

All forms of human co-operation or communication involve following some kind of agreed rules, conventions or laws. Societies are necessarily rule-governed: otherwise they would not be societies, but collections of isolated individuals. The size and complexity of most societies are such that some people have to make up rules for others who have not the time, the talent or perhaps the desire to do so. Hence a ruling class or power élite is inevitable. Moreover, the expertise and length of tenure required for efficient rule-making and administration are such that most advanced societies claim, at least, to choose members of the élite on their merits, and allow them a semi-permanent status. Hence the power élite is a permanent class, in the sense that it would not be a permanent class if officials were appointed by lot, or if they were only allowed to hold office for a day.

The existence of a permanent class in this sense is not necessarily odious to the egalitarian, since this is parallel to the existence of any class of experts—doctors, economists, lawyers, etc.—who have a particular job to do, and to whose expertise we entrust certain parts of our lives. But the egalitarian distrusts the power élite more than other experts, because the élite's mandate covers a wider area and because it can be enforced. Hence the egalitarian fears that, in such a situation, the wills and desires of individuals are likely to get lost. The mandate of the élite can only be to implement these wills and desires, not to override them, for that would be to deny intrinsic equality altogether: and hence the chief danger is that the élite should be out of touch with the people. What the people want, how they feel, how they see themselves, what they resent, what they fear—all these must be known and taken to heart by the élite. He also fears the natural consequences of such a lack of communication: briefly, that the élite may come to behave as if its members were a superior sort of person.

There seems little doubt that the egalitarian's distrust is often well founded. Thus, to take one obvious example, it is often said that the mere size of the modern sovereign state precludes effective communication, a fact which is sincerely bemoaned by genuine democrats and which pretended democrats pretend to bemoan. But, first, this is a problem which affects other societies besides the sovereign state—schools, universities, armies, towns, etc.: and, secondly, size does not always correlate with effective communication. Thus it would be perfectly possible to determine the wills and desires of the people in England, more efficiently than was done in classical Athens, by a kind of two-way television system, whereby questions were flashed on our television screens, and one could press a red button for 'yes' and a green for 'no'. We could use this to find out public feeling on questions like race prejudice, sexual morality, crime and punishment, the distribution of wealth, and so on. No doubt there might be better systems: but my point here is that we ought to, but do not, demand any such system at all. The authorities may well feel that administration is easier if they are not embarrassed by a proper knowledge of what the public feel and think. But if so, they must be resisted. It is reasonable to check *interference* by the public with the administrators, because otherwise they could not do their job: but it is never reasonable to check knowledge of the public will.

Against this it can be argued that once you allow the public to make its will known, it will take the bit between its teeth and begin to interfere with the administration, so that chaos ensues. This argument seems to me dishonest, and proceeds from a tacit denial of intrinsic equality which leads one to talk as if one were a member of the élite and 'the public' were inferiors: more precisely, as if the élite *had a super-mandate to decide the extent of its other mandates*. It is very easy to fall victim to the temptation to talk in this way. Thus I wrote at the end of the paragraph above: 'It is reasonable to check *interference* by the public with the administrators . . .' but this does not say who is to do the checking, and I may well have temporarily identified myself with the administrators, and given them the right to check 'the public' if *they* thought it reasonable. But this is a mistake. It is reasonable for 'the public'—that is, for all of us—to check our own interference: and it may even be reasonable for us to give the administrators a mandate to check our interference, withhold information from us in the interests of security, and so on. But the mandate has to be clearly seen to proceed from *us*: the élite cannot arrogate it or assume its existence.

It is important to be clear on this point, if only because we here stand in the middle of a dispute which has long been conducted in misleading terms. A question which people are very fond of asking, and which might be represented as 'Is government a matter for experts, or everybody's business?', is misleading because it might mean:

(a) 'Do we need experts in government?' or 'Does governing well involve special skills?', in which case the answer is obviously 'Yes': or (b) 'Have some people, who possess special skills, the right to dictate the values and behaviour of other people who do not have these skills?' to which the answer is 'No'. One can *call in* an expert and follow his advice, whether in government or any other field: but then one is not being dictated to, but being advised. This is what is meant by saying that the expert has a mandate.

Of course there are many cases, of which perhaps the case of government is sometimes one, where it is impossible to clarify a mandate beyond a certain point. It could be argued—indeed, I think that a firm believer in intrinsic equality would have to argue—that a parent's right to dictate his child's behaviour rests not upon the incompetence of the child to decide his own destiny (for that would be to foist our own judgements on a rational being), but upon a mandate given by the child. The child may be represented as entering into some kind of contract, whereby the parent feeds him, clothes him, and looks after him generally, and in return for this the child relinquishes the right to decide his own destiny.[1] Towards the age of adolescence this

1. This is, of course, grotesque as a psychological description, and is intended as an outline only of the moral justification of what happens.

mandate may become less absolute: but, because the child or adolescent cannot adequately communicate what sort of mandate he wants (or may not even be clear in his own mind), the parent may have to guess. Similarly the ruler of a very backward people, who cannot clearly communicate their own wishes, may have to make up his mind, on insufficient evidence, how far his people would want his powers to extend. Personal relationships with neurotics and other indecisive people present the same problems. But here again we must distinguish clearly between the cases of (a) the person who *cannot* tell you what he wants and what mandate he gives you (so that you have to guess), (b) the person who can tell you but is prevented from doing so by bad communications which are at least partly your fault, and (c) the person whom you do not allow to make up his own mind for himself because you think him incompetent to do so. The egalitarian will not tolerate cases (b) and (c), but is prepared to admit (a). He would also claim that case (a) is far rarer than most authorities are willing to admit.

The general principles which authorities should observe amount, in practice, to a few rules which are not intellectually very complex but which are rarely kept. First, the individual wants to know what is going on. He wants to be treated as a person, not as a pawn: and the minimal condition of treating someone as a person is that you should inform him of what you are doing to him. Competent army commanders know this very well, and take pains to ensure that their soldiers are treated as equals to the extent of being told what they are to do and why they are to do it, so that they at least have the chance of identifying with the commander and participating in a co-operative effort: and the same holds good for any context.

Secondly, the authorities must give people what they want and not what the authorities think good for them. It may be that a particular picture presented by the establishment is in fact more reasonable than the picture entertained by the underprivileged: thus, it is arguable that the poor are more blessed than the rich, and that it is nicer to draw a good salary as an artisan with no responsibility than to be the artisan's harassed employer. Also a mini car may be more practicable than a Rolls-Royce, and a plain girl may make a better wife than a beautiful one. But arguments of this sort will not do. First, the arguments are advanced by the authorities, who may be suspected of having vested interest in the values which they advance as reasonable; one might think: 'If he really believes it is better to be poor, or to be a worker rather than an employer, why doesn't he practise what he preaches?' And, secondly, even if the arguments are reasonable, nobody has the right to impose his values on anybody else.

Thirdly, the authorities must not bribe, flatter, cajole, or indoctrinate a person to adopt the élite's values if these are not really his own. It is very easy for an authority, by a calculated system of rewards and punishments, an indoctrinatory form of education and the propagation of a particular code or ethos, consciously or unconsciously to persuade the underprivileged or ambitious to change their values in favour of the values of the establishment. The method can be summarised in the form: 'If you behave yourself by our standards, and think as we do, you can have some of our privileges.' This is the father speaking to his child. The objections to it are not just logical—that the establishment is not a father and people are not children—but also moral—that such talk encourages us to behave as if they were. It prolongs, rather than tries to cure, our tendency to regress to a child-like posture.

Fourthly, the élite must be functional rather than privileged: and those who go into it must be seen to be qualified, in some way or other, for their jobs. This seems truistic: but it is not clear that the truism is universally accepted. We are uncertain about what tests should be applied to would-be kings, Prime Ministers, bishops, company directors, headmasters, and so on, and consequently apt to accept that certain kinds of people should do these jobs *as of right*. Thus we may contrast the view that the élite should be, so to speak, a *dynastic* body, whose powers follow automatically from their birth, wealth, or social position, with the view that they should be selected by empirical tests.

In some cases these two criteria may coincide. We may think that the best qualification for a king is, precisely, that he is the eldest son of the last king: this may be the

G

best test we can produce. But in general this coincidence is unlikely, and one is struck by apparent inconsistencies. Thus it is odd, to say the least, that administrative civil servants in England are selected by the most arduous and careful objective tests, whereas potential members of parliament are hardly tested at all: they cannot be criminals or certified lunatics, but they can be very stupid, very pre-judiced, or very neurotic. Those of us who are anxious to defend existing traditions can, of course, make plenty of points that at least mitigate the inconsistency. First, the tests which we now use for measuring intelligence, prejudice, sanity, determination and so on are by no means perfect: just as a test in terms of school performance might elimin-nate Hitler but might also eliminate Churchill, so an I.Q. test might (though this is highly unlikely) throw out an occa-sional genius along with the morons. Secondly, it could be argued that we do in fact have tests of a more subtle and efficient kind. If you want a President in the U.S.A. that can cope with tough-minded foreign dictators, the man who can fight his way through American politics with enough force and skill actually to win the presidential elec-tion may be the best man for the job—or a better man than one who might defeat him in I.Q. tests and other similar examinations. Similarly, the *acceptability* of potential M.P.s to their party caucuses and to the electorate may be the most important criterion of an efficient M.P.

A considerable increase in the use of objective tests, how-ever, seems desirable. This is, of course, to assume that these tests exist or can be devised: but I think this is a reason-able assumption. The truth is surely that using objective tests feels as if we were relinquishing our powers of choice. The unreliability of interviews does not worry interviewers, be-cause interviewers like the system as it is: they enjoy the power. Selecting people for jobs is a great source of pleasure for the selectors; just as headmasters often enjoy writing a damning testimonial for boys they dislike and a laudatory one for their favourites. We know very well how fallible human judgement is in such cases.

Egalitarians commonly say, and with some truth, that the establishment is unfairly selected by co-opting members of a particular social class, family background, or income bracket, and is hence a self-sustaining institution. But in their desire to see rewards and privileges fairly distributed, they often lose sight of the notion of qualification for function. Thus at the time of writing many complain that too high a proportion of the élite come from élite educational establishments: that too many people from Oxford and Cambridge, for instance, as opposed to other universities, manage to get into the highest class of the civil service. Now it may be true that the civil service examinations are weighted (deliberately or unconsciously) in favour of Oxbridge candidates, without regard to their efficiency: but it may also be true that those who complain wish to weight them in favour of other candidates, equally without regard to their efficiency: the criterion of acceptability can cut both ways. It is alleged that the citizens of a town in the U.S.A., having elected a Negro as mayor for one year, dared not elect a white man in subsequent years for fear of being accused of race prejudice.

2

Class Distinction

There are two senses in which class distinctions are inevitable, and two in which they are not. They are inevitable (a) in that, within the context of any one competive activity, some people will be ranked higher than others: and (b) in that people have different tastes, and will hence tend to form groups based on similarities among group-members. These are not very worrying: nobody minds losing in one context, so long as he does not lose in all contexts and is hence counted as generally 'inferior'; and nobody minds men playing cricket or women having tea-parties together, so long as these do not represent the activities of a 'superior' class. What we might object to is (i) there being an order of precedence which ranks one group higher than another in all contexts, or in too many contexts: or (ii) the particular criteria of similarity which define this 'superior' class. When we talk of 'class distinction' from within a particular society, we usually mean one of these two things. Either we object to the envy, snobbishness, pride and so on which arise from the mere existence of a class élite: or we object to the criteria by which the élite are selected. Thus a dislike of English class distinction might be a dislike of the 'class feeling' current in England, or a dislike of the *kind* of classes that exist in England, which would be very different from those which exist among the Hopi Indians or in the Vatican. Those two objections are closely connected, but I will try to deal with them in order.

(i) It is important to see why the existence of a 'superior' class is not, as some have argued, entirely inevitable. Much depends here on what exactly we are objecting to when we decry 'class distinction' in this sense. Thus our objection may be to the existence of an upper class which is traditionally accepted as superior, but which (in our view) ought not to be so accepted. We might not object to an upper class who satisfied what we took to be the right criteria: those, say, who were the most conscientious or loving or saintly. If these qualities represented our own ideals, we might well accept such a class as worthy to be admired and emulated: we should accept them as better *people*. Alternatively, the criterion of selection might change the élite so rapidly that there would be no permanent group as a target for envy. For instance, if wealth or honours constantly changed hands, as a result of throwing dice or cutting cards. we should hardly be able to speak of *an* élite at all. Individuals could be kings for a day, or millionaires for a month. The only class of people to envy would be the class of lucky people: and this is not a permanent class, since no one is permanently lucky.

I do not think, however, that either of these possibilities meets any existing practical situation: nor are they the arguments on which the egalitarian would rely in pointing to the possibility of reducing or abolishing class distinction. His real argument depends on the desirability and practicability of fitting social norms and arrangements to people, rather than vice versa. To take a practical example, let us suppose that you are running a boarding house at a boys' school. If you wished to promote equality and cut down class distinctions, you would try to define success, and to arrange the symbols of prestige, in such a way that every boy could shine at some activity and have some kind of prestige. As a beginning, for instance, you might award 'colours' or other prestige symbols not just to those who were good at games or work, but to those who did well at music or carpentry, or even collecting dirty milk bottles. You would start by finding out what each boy could contribute, and arrange your prestige activities accordingly.

But you would find, of course, that external pressures or internal necessity gave certain functions a particular importance. Thus for most schools to survive and flourish, external social pressures necessitate that enough scholarships should be gained, enough football matches won, and so on: and similarly, to keep the house running properly, you would need a number of prefects who are allowed to give orders to other people. Hence, unless you did something about it, you would find a natural 'upper class' consisting of prefects, scholarship winners and athlocrats, and a natural 'lower class' consisting of the badly behaved and incompetent. However, you could compensate for this in various ways, all of which amount to denying that these natural pressures had any real value *within* the society, whilst admitting that the society as a whole had to take account of them. First, you could as it were over-compensate those whose contributions brought them no natural prestige, giving extra rewards to those who collected milk bottles, and assuming that scholarship-winners were sufficiently rewarded by the outside world. Secondly, you could ensure that there was plenty of communication between possible élites, such as the prefects, and the rest: so that they would not come to be regarded as superior *people*, but simply ordinary individuals doing a particular job. Thirdly, you could apply your sanctions to the badly behaved without implying any kind of absolute moral value in the social norms which you enforce: so that, again, you would not suggest that the badly behaved were inferior people, but rather that they were individuals who were unsuccessful at following one set of rules, though they might be very successful in other fields. Lastly, you could arrange for as many non-competitive contexts of co-operation as possible, in which questions of individual prestige did not arise.

This suggests that it is false to regard social inequality as logically inevitable. In practice a certain amount of it may be inevitable in that our arrangements to avert it will no doubt always be to some extent defective. All societies are subject to external and internal pressures, and all have their own norms and sanctions: inequality and class distinction may flow from both of these causes. But members of society also have the power to adjust the situation in the ways I have roughly outlined: a power which they will wish to use if they reflect sufficiently upon the ideal of intrinsic equality and its importance. Moreover, it must be observed that non-sovereign societies like schools, being founded and maintained for a particular purpose, are much more liable to specific pressures and the necessity of specific norms than are sovereign states. For it is inappropriate to speak of 'the purpose' of the sovereign state: we can make our society fulfil whatever purposes we like, and provided we have taken care of the necessity of economic survival and defence against other societies, one of the chief purposes which we ought to make our society fulfil is the maintenance of equality.

(ii) In considering the particular criteria of class that prevail in any society, we need first to develop some of the points made about competitive games and social rewards in Part One. We saw there that the egalitarian is always somewhat hostile to contexts of competition, because (briefly) no set of rules can be regarded as ideally fair, except possibly those which reward only the direction of moral choice and effort. In principle the egalitarian would like to see nothing but contexts of co-operation. In practice, however, he has to face the hard fact that there are some things which people passionately want for themselves, and about which they are not prepared to be co-operative. Some passionate desires, such as perhaps some sexual desires, could in principle be met non-competitively by making the desired objects much more available: thus (to put it bluntly) if anybody was prepared to sleep with anybody else when asked, it is conceivable that the intensity of competition in this field would be much diminished. The egalitarian will always attempt to avoid such difficulties by this general method, i.e. by persuading people to co-operate rather than compete; but, as our example shows, he is not likely to meet with immediate success. Moreover, some objects of desire are by their nature limited: not everybody can be the possessor of the Mona Lisa, or Prime Minister, or Miss England 1965.

These passionate wants might make us react in two different ways. First we might be so envious of those that achieve their desires, that we decided to scrap competition for them altogether. We could do this (a) by abolishing the objects or sharing them—we abolish Miss England competitions and the office of Prime Minister, or we allow everyone to own the Mona Lisa for a few minutes: or (b) by turning the competition into a game of chance—we choose the Prime Minister by lot, or have a raffle for the Mona Lisa. We shall probably do (a) if we dislike the whole idea of anyone being fortunate enough to gain the object of his desires, and (b) if we are jealous of whatever talents or merits allow a person to gain the object in open competition. The first leads to uniformity, the second to lotteries.

Alternatively, since we ourselves strongly desire these things we might precisely for this reason feel cheated by any suggestion that they should be abolished or distributed by lot. We might feel that we want the chance to compete for them, even perhaps if we do not feel confident about having the talents required for winning. If those who want these things most should have them, which might seem a reasonable principle, then the game should be kept open: we can work hard at improving our talents and in general leave no stone unturned to gain our objective. We should at least be able to *try*: whereas if the matter is a mere lottery, even that is taken from us.

What weight should be given to such considerations is —assuming we are clear about our values—a matter of sociological and psychological fact. The egalitarian will not try to settle practical questions of this sort by refer- ence to any absolute principle of desert or justice. He will consider how much competition people desire, how much is in fact necessary to provide incentives, and so on: and the rules which he advocates will follow from these empirical facts, rather than being derived from tradition or accepted intuitively. As he will appreciate, the egalitarian principle, which advocates rules that reward capacities which every- one has to some extent (such as the ability to make an effort or work hard), is not one that we can immediately put into effect without regard for psychological consequences. Games of this sort, which are played in a mobile society, may place an intolerable strain on the players. The *extent* of the competitive arena, as well as its location, must depend on what they can stand. By increasing the number of com- petitors—and this is usually the practical effect of increased 'equality of opportunity'—we may in fact diminish our communications: the more competition, the less co-operation.

In a highly stratified society, based on a caste system which is traditionally accepted, individuals may feel more secure and communicate better within their own caste—or status-groups, if not outside them.

Assuming that the psychological facts do not tell too heavily against him, however, the egalitarian will seek to implement the policy described in Part One: that is, in so far as he is compelled to allow competition at all, he will want the rules to favour capacities that we all possess. In practice this comes down to setting up the kind of game *which can be won in as many different ways as possible*, and in which the criteria of desert are not too closely attached to any one particular set of talents. Thus, suppose winning one game consists of getting possession of a beautiful woman. Then we could imagine two sets of rules: (i) you can only win by being very rich: (ii) you can win by being rich, or clever, or handsome, or witty, or attentive. Now whilst it is true in one sense that *no more* people can win under system (ii) than under system (i), yet system (ii) obviously brings more people into the game. If we play system (i), then if I am not rich and cannot get rich I shall give up hope. But if we play (ii), then even if I am not rich I can try to be clever or witty: if I am not clever or witty I can try to be attentive, and so on. Thus although in one sense the egalitarian cannot, whatever system he arranges, give any more people a chance to *win* (since there is a limited number of winners), he can give more people *hope*.

We may now apply these points to a practical situation. Social classes in England, and in most technologically developed countries, depend ultimately on money. This is not to say that money defines class: only that it is usually predictable that, given time, the rich will have more status then the poor. They acquire this status by intermediary methods which depend on money: amongst these are going to the best sort of school, learning to speak with the best sort of accent, entertaining and being entertained by the best sort of people, and having the best sort of status-symbols. It is virtually inevitable that these should depend on money, at least in any kind of *laissez-faire* economy, for 'the best sort' of anything has a scarcity value, and will

H

therefore be expensive. If it does not have a scarcity value it is no longer 'the best sort'.

I am not, of course, saying that statements about a person's class can be translated into statements about his financial position. 'Upper class' does not *mean* 'rich'. What it does mean depends on the society, and even on the individual speaker within a society. Thus in England birth, manner of speaking, style of life, type of education, and many other things go to form the criteria of class. Nevertheless, in an open-market economy, money is by far the most important *causal* factor for class membership in the generally accepted social sense of 'class'. Moreover, because the upper class are (almost by definition) admired for all their characteristics, and not just their wealth, these other characteristics are often financial assets. To have been to the right school, or to be well connected, or even to speak with the right accent, are valuable in the open market.

The chief reason why the underprivileged object to class distinction based on this criterion is that membership of the upper class gives people a much better chance to get most of the things that people strongly desire. These things boil down, in practice, to three categories: getting the possessions you want, getting the girls (or men) you want, and getting the jobs you want. We must distinguish between the mere snobbery of a person who wants to belong to the upper class as such, and the feeling of an underprivileged person who is aware of certain hard and bitter facts: that he cannot have a spacious house, go for expensive holidays, afford the best doctors or lawyers, drink the best wines, or sail his own yacht: that the most attractive girls (and men) tend to move amongst the upper classes, and that he has little chance of meeting them and less of marrying them: and (since many jobs are not awarded on merit) that he is not likely to be sufficiently known or sufficiently acceptable to get the jobs he wants from those that control them.

To distinguish snobbery from more genuine feeling is not easy. Thus the sexual attractiveness of upper-class girls may partly derive from the mere fact that they are upper class, rather than the facts that upper-class girls tend to acquire more poise and confidence from their social position, and (by natural selection, since the rich have a better chance of marrying pretty girls) to be generally more desirable. Similarly it is not clear whether people want to speak with an upper-class accent because this is how the upper classes speak, or because this accent is objectively more pleasant than Cockney or a West Country burr. But it is at least plain that the underprivileged may have a genuine cause for resentment, rather than merely being snobbish. Moreover, if the upper classes, because they have more money, also have more characteristics which are in themselves desirable, such as more culture, or leader-like qualities, or a stronger sense of responsibility, then the resentment of the under-privileged will be more, not less, justifiable.

Now suppose we change the criteria of class, and grade ourselves according to intelligence or academic ability. Would this meet their objection? The answer would depend on how many privileges were now gained by this new upper class of intelligentsia. If these privileges were largely symbolic—if the intelligentsia were merely accorded defer-ence, admiration and so on—then the underprivileged might not object too much: though they could still claim that this class system tended to isolate the intelligentsia and remove them from the arena of common communication. But if the intelligentsia received more possessions, more attractive women and better jobs as a result of their class, the ob-jections of the underprivileged would not have been met at all.

The advantage of the criterion of money over such cri-teria as intelligence, good looks or noble birth is that the former allows of more movement from one class to another than the latter. As we saw earlier, we want to get as many people into the competitive game as possible: and where-as I cannot do anything about being stupid, ugly, or of lowly birth, I can always try to make money. As long as there are plenty of ways of making money, I can reason-ably hope to succeed if I try hard enough and want it enough: and in this respect the values of the market-place are not to be despised. The alternative might be some kind of rigid caste system, based either on individual character-istics that I cannot change and that may well be hereditary, such as I.Q. or good looks. But if we defend the criterion for this reason, we must make sure it works. We must not make the possession of money dependent on any sort of caste system: and on this basis, we cannot defend inherited wealth or financial rewards for talents which the individual cannot help having or not having, such as I.Q. These may be defensible by other kinds of arguments; but the egalitarian will not accept arguments based on alleged merit or desert, because for him desert must be defined in terms of people's wants. He will accept any sound argument from the necessity for incentives, but there is no certainty that the facts support this argument sufficiently to justify existing inequalities of wealth, and the class system which derives from them.

In any case, there are other arguments against the use of money as a criterion, besides the fact that it deprives too many people of their desires. First, some of these desires would normally be counted as needs. It seems indefensible that the best doctors, the best lawyers, or the best schools be reserved for the rich. Even if we took account of desert, and even if the rich were always thought to be the most deserving, it would still be unfair: we believe that things like medicine, education and legal aid should be distributed according to need rather than according to desert.

Secondly, even though money leaves the competitive game fairly open, it does not leave it open enough. Not very many people have the chance or the talent to make money, particularly in a highly competitive and highly organised economy like our own: everyone does not start fair.

Thirdly, the criterion of money permits and even encourages poor communications between one class and another. There is always, perhaps, some resentment felt against exclusive groups, irrespective of their class: but when this exclusiveness is connected with the objects of desire, the resentment is increased tenfold. Thus the social segregation of the upper classes—the fact that they occupy certain quarters in towns, do not often mix socially with other classes, send their children to schools which isolate them from children of other classes, and so forth—is in itself a justifiable cause for complaint: all the more justifiable because their houses, forms of entertainment and élite schools are perhaps superior to those of other people. Money permits a class to segregate itself far more than would other criteria, such as intelligence, strength, beauty, or hard work.

Fourthly, existing inequalities in wealth permit and encourage people to compete in a form which does not particularly improve our communication. Denied to some extent of the chance of competing in wealth, people might well be forced into fields of competition which were more profitable, because more related to their personalities—to what they *are* rather than what they *have*. To compete in good taste, intelligence, physical skills, knowledge and similar things is by no means ideally desirable: but it is preferable to competing in the possession of material objects.

Finally, there is an argument of a rather more complicated kind, relating not to the disparities between social classes but the bad effects of a moneyed upper class that operate *within* that class. The argument is that money can too easily be used to isolate people from reality: and in essence it applies as much to the middle class, or any sufficiently affluent class, as to the élite. I am not speaking here of the kind of isolation which prevents the rich from knowing 'how the other half lives': still less do I suggest that wealth isolates them from 'higher' things—that they are too keen on money and not keen enough on culture or religion. The point is rather that any kind of luxury living promotes a forgetfulness of the ordinary and basic facts of life: one of which, indeed, is precisely the necessity of getting enough money to make ends meet. Wealth has the effect of cushioning the rich against these facts, and the harsh but inevitable order of priorities in human existence tends to be forgotten.

There is a very strong case for drastic revision of the distribution of wealth. We might begin naively with equalising everyone's incomes, and at least trying to keep them equal by legislating against inheritance and exploitation. We should then find that we needed incentives in order to get people to do certain jobs: but it is far from clear that those who do the top jobs would need incentives the most. The status and interest of such jobs might provide a sufficient incentive in themselves: and we might find it necessary to bribe dustmen and labourers to do their jobs, rather than bribe company directors to do theirs. In general, however, we would need to consider, first, what makes people work hard and efficiently at their jobs (as opposed to taking up the job at all): how far a rise in pay is a necessary incentive, and how far other factors play a leading part, such as the interest of the job, being one's own master, getting on well with one's fellow-workers, and many other things. Secondly, we may well think it impossible to maintain equality of wealth, since it is very difficult to prevent gifts, gambling, saving, and various economic contracts between individuals, even if we should wish to: and I have argued earlier that it *may* be psychologically misguided to do so. Nevertheless, the onus of proof in these factual issues lies on those who wish to preserve inequality: for the *prima facie* arguments in favour of a great deal more equality are very strong.

I suspect that there may be far more people who are worried about being underprivileged than there are people who want more privileges than others. They do not want to look down on others: they simply do not want to be looked down on by others. The security of having an income which is not grossly inferior to anyone else's would, I believe, more than compensate for their inability to strive for an income which is grossly superior. Plenty of people are exceptions to this generalisation, but I should guess them to be a minority: and I should also guess that far more people fall under the generalisation than they themselves might think. Given a traditional class-system based on money, it is hard to imagine oneself seeking quite different competitive aims: but almost everyone, if brought face to face with a situation where obtaining very much more money was impossible *for everybody*, would find new aims to strive for without difficulty. I suspect the general relief would be enormous: for there is a sense in which people do not really want to compete, but find themselves driven to do so. What drives them is not merely a competitive economy, but an inner compulsion from which they find it impossible to break free. 'The rat race' is well named. We are not happy with this style of life, and make uneasy jokes about it: but we remain compelled because we cannot picture anything else. From this point of view a change towards much greater equality would, in my view, prove far more acceptable than might be supposed.

What new criteria of class would then appear is quite uncertain: for we are so used to money as the ultimate criterion of class that it is not at all clear which other possible criteria would operate. If I had to guess, I should suspect that things like 'culture' and 'good taste' would be among the operative criteria: and though this sounds fairly odious, it is perhaps not quite as bad as the present situation. In any case, the abolition of wealth as virtually the only criterion of class would at least offer us the chance of replacing it by multiple criteria of some kind, and hence as it were loosen up the game. Some might seek to compete in intelligence, others in good looks, others in strength, others in style of life, others in conscientious work, and so forth. It might not be too much to hope that we should make somewhat more effort to fit these criteria to the actual abilities of people (as in my example in (i) above), rather than forcing people into the single straitjacket of money.

I am also starry-eyed enough to suppose (though there is very little evidence either way) that, once we are on a more equal footing with reference to the objects of our desires, we shall slowly learn to become less competitive and more co-operative. You cannot expect people to communicate and co-operate if they feel that they are being cheated of what they want. It is perhaps difficult for the upper classes, who are not usually wicked but are often unimaginative, to appreciate that people do feel cheated. Part of the reason for this is that, in England at least, there is still a tradition of silence and faint distaste about money in some of the more well-established upper classes: it suggests to them, as to the Roman patricians, a touch of the bourgeois. It is also difficult for the underprivileged, who have to keep their end up, to admit to the intensity of their feelings: there is a temptation for them to acquiesce in the *status quo*—if not when they are young, at least when they are old enough to have settled the main outlines of their lives. This kind of dishonesty has to be resisted if we are to make any progress. Nothing is gained by attaching blame: but one might reasonably expect more effort from the upper classes than the lower. It should be in principle more easy to understand jealousy and envy, particularly when it is reasonable, than to stop feeling it.

This kind of understanding, as we saw in the last Part, depends ultimately on the ability to identify with other people: and from this derives the most powerful argument for equality. The psychological roots of class-feeling are common to all men, in whatever social class they happen to find themselves. Without going deeply into psychoanalytic theory, it is quite easy to see that overt desires for money, status, important jobs, and all that goes with these things are instances of a more general and perhaps largely unconscious desire to be powerful or potent. Men want to have powerful cars in order to prove that they themselves are powerful: women want to prove to themselves, by such means as dress, jewellery, rank, possessions, or social position, that they are important, and can capture important men. Both seek to allay their unconscious fears that they are small, weak, inferior, impotent, still in the state of childhood, unable to assert their will and their identity.

There is nothing that cannot be used to make a demonstration of power in this way. The use of a superior intelligence, greater cultural knowledge, athletic ability, or even what may look like simple generosity, may all be motivated by a desire to exert power. Amongst more common methods are naked power over others, as in tyrants and gang leaders: power acquired by position, as in politicians and tycoons: power acquired by money, which enables one to give orders to those you employ or can influence financially: power acquired by personality, as in film stars or pop singers. A common method in past ages, and still very much alive in some societies, is to rely upon birth and family: a man thinks himself powerful because he imagines himself to incorporate the power of his ancestors: in a sense, he *is* them and has their fame and their status.

In considering what political moves may be made to alleviate these feelings, we must be guided by those methods of power-seeking which the individual takes to be important: not by those which are 'really' important. To those who have been to a well-known school it may seem incredible that many people who have fame, riches, intellectual ability and personal charm may nevertheless feel themselves impotent and inferior simply because they were educated in obscurity. Similarly to people of normal stature the efforts of

the physically undersized to compensate for their deficiency often seem grotesque: but since this factor may
play a large part in the careers of such people as Hitler and
Napoleon, we cannot solve the problem simply by telling
short people not to be silly. Since the criterion of potency
in our society is chiefly the criterion of money, there is a
strong case for economic equality: a case independent of
any considerations about the 'real' importance of money.
Toys in themselves are not important: but they become important if one child in a family is given a great many toys,
while another has hardly any. Nor is this all. For even
if we could establish that a feeling of potency depended
not upon money but upon some other thing, it is still very
likely that this other thing will need money to obtain. It
may of course not be obtainable at all except by chance, as
would be the case with good looks or a six-foot statue.
But if it is obtainable, money will probably be able to buy it.
Given money, you can create your own job, your own sur-
roundings, and your own leisure activities. To a great extent you can choose your own wife or husband, and your
own acquaintances. You can buy as much physical health
as scientists are able to sell you: and if you are still dissatis-
fied, you can buy a psychoanalyst to put you right. This brief
statement is of course psychologically naive: but there is
enough truth in it to prevent us from resting content with a
purely psychological view. For however mentally healthy
we are, everyone needs *some* method of establishing his
power and identity. The most obvious methods, which
alone are available to all but the most sophisticated, necessitate money; and if these methods are denied to a person, he
has no alternative but to feel bitter and underprivileged.
Apart from any feelings of humanity which we might
reasonably entertain towards such people, they are liable to
be dangerous. This is a truth which frequent revolutions and
other semi-violent political changes have constantly reiter-
ated, but which the overprivileged have not yet grasped. It
is for these reasons that a Marxist insight, as well as a
Freudian, is necessary for the practical egalitarian: and it is
a matter of infinite regret that both have made so little
impact even on the intelligent public. These insights have
too often been diverted into metaphysical, almost mystical,

channels. People will adhere to Marxism or Freudianism as to a political party or to a religion: and other people will in effect disregard them both, paying them only lip-service when it is plain that no serious thinker about human beings (whether in the context of politics or of personal relationships) can afford to miss the point of either. When a break-down in communication of this magnitude is left unrepaired, it is unlikely that we shall be successful in solving the problems presented by class-feeling.

3

Personal Relationships
and Equality between
the Sexes

Political rules are inevitably framed on too large a scale, and are consequently too clumsy, to cope very well with the communication on which intrinsic equality depends for much of its cash value. But we might, however, expect to find rather more detailed and delicate rules in the field of personal relationships. By 'personal relationships' I here intend to include all associations which are, at least *prima facie*, associations of equals: committees, a group of friends, a married couple, or three people sharing a flat. This field is particularly important, because the egalitarian wishes either to turn what we now call 'politics' into equality-relationships, or else to reduce politics to a series of decisions by experts about which we need not argue. In either case the result would be the same—that our chief interest lies in equality-relationships and the rules that should govern them. Thus, to use crude examples, whether we decentralise our society so that everyone can play an equal part in a number of smaller societies, or allow economists and other experts to decide about our technology whilst reserving the right to decide as equals about non-technological issues, the most important part of our lives will lie in how we handle each other as equals.

But in fact we are very much in the dark about this whole subject. Certain associations, such as marriage, are founded on some kind of contract: others, such as committees, have rules of procedure: we can think of rules of convention and good manners that govern our normal human intercourse: but here we run out of ammunition. Almost every day a book is produced about how to handle your husband or wife, how to win friends and influence people, how to think clearly and argue properly, and so on: but not much is said about equality-relationships as such. Although this is discouraging, it reinforces the point that the chief obstacle to the formulation of such rules is that we do not really want to formulate them: we prefer contexts of order and obedience rather than contexts of equality.

Communication, in the simple sense of talking to each other, depends on following rules of meaning, the rules of a language. But we extend our rule-following far beyond this. Conventional rituals and manners, even when they are not linguistically expressed, follow rules which allow us to communicate in certain ways: think of standing some- one a drink, smiling to someone in the street, or making love. These are like the rules of a game, and children have to learn them in order to become adult. Sometimes the pur- pose of such rules is simple enjoyment, as in a game: and I have argued earlier that communication has no final purpose beyond itself. But sometimes the rules are directed towards a different end: committees wish to arrive at a correct decision, we argue (sometimes) in order to find the truth, we play in an orchestra in order to give a good render- ing of a piece of music.

This is the first distinction to be drawn, the distinction between games which have no ulterior purpose, and rule- governed activities (we have called them 'games' on the understanding that they may, despite the name, be very serious) which are directed to some external end. In prac- tice the distinction often becomes blurred. Committees, schools, and businesses are supposed to exist for specific purposes: to reach decisions, turn out good pupils, or sell oil. Yet we are all familiar with the regrettable tendency of all such organisations to relapse into following rules which in reality serve only to sustain and support themselves. In a word, they turn into clubs. Some people sit on committees in order to get things done: others just like being there and talking. Phrases like 'It's for the good of the school' may refer to the benefit of the pupils who are the end product, but only too often refers to the interests of those who run the school.

But this is only one of many distinctions. In all contexts

of communication, we have to ask ourselves 'What game are we playing?' Consider a familiar situation, which may be represented in four stages. First, a group of people talk to each other in a fairly casual way: they gossip, swap stories, exchange information, and so on. Then an argument arises: and for a time they remain reasonable and endeavour to find out the truth. Then members of the group begin to make personal comments and say things like 'Why do you feel so strongly about it?' or 'Your father taught you that, didn't he?' Finally they lose their tempers, and begin throwing plates at each other. Now these are four different games, each of which (if played properly) could be justifiable. The first is played for pure pleasure. The second is played with a view to discovering truth: an interruption by somebody who was still trying to play the first game—perhaps by inserting an irrelevant anecdote or piece of information—would hold up the second game. In the third game the players are indulging in a kind of amateur psychoanalysis: they are no longer concerned with the truth about the subject under discussion, but with the truth about their motives and feelings. In the fourth game they are letting off steam at each other: and perhaps it would be preferable if they did it in the form of some real game of a semi-violent nature, like football, which would save the plates from being broken.

Now it is likely that, if only we were aware of the variety of games that we can play, we should be able to formulate our rules without much difficulty. Thus we all know that in rational discussion we should not gossip, or be personal, or lose our tempers. If it were clear, and agreed beforehand, what game we were supposed to be playing at any one time, and if everyone knew that other games would be played later, our communications would be much improved. Thus if I know that from 2 to 2.30 I am supposed to be arguing, from 2.30 to 3 we are going to investigate each other's motives, and from 3 to 3.30 let off steam by throwing plates or playing football, I am much more likely to argue properly. I would not even object to a fairly tight set of rules, whereby warning bells would be rung if I raised my voice above a certain pitch, or slight electric shocks were given to me if I lost my temper.

Such arrangements seem artificial and absurd: but there is a bad as well as a good reason for thinking them so. The bad reason is that we suppose our communications to be so satisfactory that we do not need them: and this I do not think that anyone who desires to communicate seriously with his fellow-beings can honestly believe. It is true that, given enough love, or good-will, or whatever we care to call it, in a marriage or a friendship or any other association, we do not need explicit rules. But, first, we do not find very many of these ideal relationships: we know perfectly well how much we suffer from quarrels, resentment and misunderstanding. And secondly, although relationships of love and goodwill do not use rules explicitly, yet they still use them: indeed they use more of them than unsatisfactory relationships. We are accustomed to think of love as a kind of magic, which abolishes the need for rules: but the truth is that love is *defined* by the proper following of rules. People who love each other play one game at a time, and play it well: they respond instinctively to the demand of that particular game, and keep its rules. Thus learning to love is, precisely, learning to play different communication-games; and if we cannot do this by nature or instinct, we had better learn it consciously and deliberately.

The good reason for being suspicious of over-formalisation is that it may make insufficient allowance for what we actually feel: this point is parallel to, indeed virtually the same as, what we said in the last section about the desire to compete. The importance of behaviour that is not consciously rule-governed—that is, of spontaneity—is that what we feel emerges thereby. When a man loses his temper in an argument, or a woman becomes personal, there is a sense in which they are saying something which has to be said. Our rules must not be so tight as to repress it altogether. For the whole point of having rules at all is to communicate: and we cannot do this if our feelings do not emerge—we would have lost the *material* of our communication, and preserved only the skeletal forms.

But granted this, there is no reason why we should not make our rules as sophisticated and finely adjusted as possible. We may take an example of one particular game, the taking of a group decision: imagine that four people agree to go to the same cinema together and want to decide which cinema to go to. They regard each other as equals, so that the wants of each carry equal weight: and the point of the game is to provide the maximum of pleasure all round. Now it may be that they identify with each other so well and A is happiest if B goes to the cinema that B would choose for himself, and so on: but not all groups are so fraternal. (Even if they were, there is another more selfish kind of pleasure to be taken into account besides the pleasure of doing what somebody else wants to do, i.e. the pleasure directly given to each individual by the film itself.) Then they might allow each individual ten points, any number of which he can assign to any film. He can use the points either as plus points, for the films he positively wants to see, or as minus points, in order to mark down the films he would actively dislike seeing. The film with the most points is chosen.

It might be possible to find a better decision-procedure, and in any case this will no doubt seem a trivial example. But just how trivial is it? We are all familiar with incompetent decision-procedures in the course of which individuals profess themselves willing to do anything that anybody else wants to do, or try to bully the others into doing what they want, of feeling uncomfortable when they actually do whatever it is, in case other people would have preferred to do something else. If we take seriously the notion of treating each other as equals, it seems to me that some such procedure is essential. Far from being an unfortunate necessity, it is something which we should all seek after and try to improve on.

We observed earlier that the notions of liberty and interference were in themselves incoherent: and we can now see more clearly how they depend for their content on clearly defined rules. There are plenty of occasions on which individuals prefer master-slave relationships: but there are also plenty of occasions on which individuals want equality-relationships but do not know how to get them. They want neither to be interfered with, nor to interfere, neither to have pressure put on them, nor to put pressure on others. But what counts as 'interference' or 'pressure' is wholly defined by the rules of particular games. In an argument-game, throwing plates is interference: but in a plate-throwing game, it is not. Some people hate all forms of quarrelling, and regard even a cross look as a form of pressure or emotional black-mail: others enjoy such games. All that matters is that we should pick those games which are profitable for communication, and be clear which games we are playing at any one time.

Equality between the sexes is a classic example of the need for these principles. Female emancipation is an eccentricity, almost wholly confined to modern technological societies. Elsewhere it has generally been held that women, though undoubtedly superior to children, animals, and furniture, should for some purposes be classified with them and not with men. They might have rights, but they were not equals. Granted the validity of a criterion of rationality which favours the male sex, such as that used by Aristotle, there is much to be said for this point of view: but the egalitarian has to recognise the fact that women have wills and purposes, and are people: and he will consequently want them treated as equals.

Unfortunately we have here a model case of individual psychology failing to meet the demands of egalitarian principle. For though women in our society may be emancipated in the sense of having the vote, being equal with men in the eyes of the law, being allowed to own property, take up careers and so forth, most honest women will admit that they are not psychologically emancipated. They do not desire to be treated as equals. In the last resort, they want the wills of men—or of a particular man—to count for more than their own. They may wish to be treated with respect, valued, loved and cherished and deferred to on occasion: but they do not want an equal voice in decision-making. Nor is it clear that men wish to give them an equal voice.

Even those women who can sincerely deny this would admit, I think, that they would find difficulty in implementing an egalitarian policy. Some of the difficulties may still be economic: women are more tied by children, they may have fewer educational opportunities, and there may be more prejudices against them in their careers. Some may be the result of social prejudice: unmarried women may still have less status than wives, all women are conventionally expected to behave in certain 'feminine' ways, and so forth. But some are plainly psychological. A proper egalitarian policy would involve a considerable reorientation of the female mind. Instead of playing a passive role, and allowing their lives to revolve around men (together with the children and home which men provide), they would have to be willing to take the initiative as much as men: they would ask men out for dates, pay for themselves, and be prepared to make the first sexual advances. Determination and masterfulness would be expected from them as much as from men: and the whole passive, admiration-seeking apparatus of clothes, cosmetics and coquetry would have to be abandoned, or at least severely modified.

Much of this is not worrying. No egalitarian will object to a woman playing different roles, having different interests, or behaving in different ways from a man. All that he objects to is inequality in the weighting of wills and desires. But it is precisely at this point that the psychology of the two sexes lets us down. If women want to be told what to do, and men want to tell them, intrinsic equality vanishes. There will be a strong sense in which women never grow up, and men never allow them to grow up. Some would argue that this is inevitable, being due either to physiological factors, or to psychological factors of so deep a kind that we cannot hope to overcome them. But it would be premature to despair: there are, after all, some women who like to be treated as equals and some men who like to treat them so: the thing is not impossible.

Like all problems in personal relationships, this problem depends for its solution on clarifying the rules of the game: and in particular clarifying the kind of contracts, formal or informal, which men and women make. For example, a date is sometimes regarded as a contract with fairly well-known rules. The man asks the girl to go out, he decides where to go and what to do, he pays for it, and takes the girl home at the end. Within broad limits, he is allowed to behave as he wishes. The girl contracts to accept the man's decision, to dress up nicely for him, smile brightly, and in general follow his conversational lead: she may also contract to be kissed good night. There are circles in which these rules, and even more clear-cut rules than these, are understood and followed. But very often it is not clear to either side what the terms of the contract are. Both parties may have disappointed expectations. In the more formal contract of a marriage, the disappointments are even greater, because the expectations are greater. The wife did not realise that she would be expected to stay at home almost every evening, or sleep with her husband whenever he wanted to: the husband did not realise that his wife would object to his going out with his men friends, or that he would be expected to help with the washing-up. In particular, the sexual expectations of each (if they have not taken the precaution of clarifying the rules of this particular game before marriage) are apt to be bitterly disappointed: for this is an activity of great importance to each, but the rules of which are even more rarely clarified than most rules.

It does not matter to the egalitarian what contracts are made. The financial, working, social, and sexual areas of married life may be governed by any rules that the couple agree on. People may marry on the understanding that the husband is allowed to spend all the spare money on himself, and sleep with other women if he wants to: or on the understanding that the wife can rule the home entirely, and is allowed to nag her husband if he looks at another woman or fails to change his shirt every day. As long as the rules are agreed and kept, the wills of each are implemented. Here too we must not think that to draw up a careful and detailed statement of the rules, or the development of more sophisticated rules in the light of experience, indicates a lack of love: quite the contrary. Yet this is rarely done.

It is not done before marriage, because the simplest form of communication—honest discussion—is largely lacking. Whether through fear, a feeling of being vulnerable, a cunning desire to gain their own ends, or sheer stupidity, most men and women are not honest with each other. I am not using 'honest' in any very sophisticated sense here. They simply do not signal their wants and intentions clearly. A recording of what went on in a person's head when talking to an attractive person of the opposite sex would be utterly unlike anything that the person indicated by word, gesture, or any other conventional sign: and perhaps I shall be forgiven for saying that a recording of a woman's real thoughts would be even more surprising than a recordings of a man's.

A popular theory is designed to meet this criticism, roughly to the effect that an agreed system of signalling 'would take all the mystery and excitement out of it'. Certainly we must be careful not to over-formalise; first, as we saw earlier, because we must preserve spontaneity: and secondly, because at least one set of rules must fulfil the purpose of allowing each party simply to find out what the other is like, by trial and error. But these points hardly meet the case. Spontaneity is just what is lacking between sexes, and one good way of finding out what people are like is to talk with them honestly. If people want to discover each other, they must communicate by some rules: if they prefer the 'mystery and excitement' of not discovering (until it is too late), then of course they will do better not to communicate at all. Nor am I convinced that knowledge lessens either mystery or excitement: and since the depths of the human mind will certainly not be wholly plumbed in our time, the mysterious and exciting unknown will always be with us in sufficient measure.

One suspects that this popular theory is itself a dishonest defence against acknowledging what we all know to be true: namely that we all suffer (or, if we have by now sufficiently deadened ourselves, have suffered in the past) from the anxiety and insecurity which comes from this hopelessly inadequate form of communication. Having broken through the more formal conventions of our fathers and grandfathers which provided adequate security if not adequate scope, we badly need to create new conventions of our own: conventions devised to increase both security and scope. We must, of course, be careful not to go faster than people can manage. (Some hold, not absurdly, that unless we accept at least some degree of inferiority for women the sexual potency of men would be severely curtailed, to the detriment of both parties.) But we can at least frame rules which will enable us to make some conscious and deliberate progress towards relationships of equality.

One learns most easily to be an equal by taking part in some context which is rule-governed in a fairly obvious sense: in an office, in the army, in team games, and in communal projects generally. For psychological as well as social reasons, women do not take easily to such contexts, either at school or in adult life. Their chief desire is to have a man, a home, and children, *of their own*. To suggest that women should take more part in the kind of rule-governed contexts that men indulge in would not be wholly absurd, but is perhaps at present a slightly forlorn hope. It would have no merit in itself—people are entitled to choose their own contexts, and to insist that women be made to play team games and commit themselves to careers would be to insist on a wholly unnecessary kind of equality. The value of the suggestion would lie solely in the possibility that it might give women more practice in learning what an equality-relationship was. For, since their own ends can only be achieved by a relationship of some kind with a man, they must at least learn to make it an equality-relationship. This again is not to say that they should not be content with cooking and looking after children while the man earns their living. But the woman must appreciate that she is under some kind of contract, and has a part which she must play. She may devote her life to being ancillary to the man, attending to his mental and physical wants and comfort: or she may do a job as he does. But whatever the contract, she has a métier: and it is important that she should be clear about what that métier is. This is a necessary form of equality, as it is a necessary form of justice.

Most twentieth-century women, who are not brought up to act as ancillaries to men, would find it as hard to accept a position of absolute inferiority as to accept a relationship of equality. Moreover, if a woman is regarded solely as an ancillary, and is given the kind of mutual contract that existed between a knight and his armour-bearer, or a lord of the manor and his serf, the woman will inevitably tend to lose all power of making decisions and perhaps all will to make them: and hence we should regress to a view whereby women were not regarded as people in the full sense. This the egalitarian cannot tolerate, for it means that his chief line of defence is abandoned. But he will in all cases prefer a contract which suits the needs of the parties concerned (even if this means that the woman adopts a large ancillary role), to one which is not clearly formulated at all. In most sexual contracts today, either one (or both) of the parties has not got a contract clearly in mind at all: or they both have a contract clearly in mind, but it is a different contract in each case—they have not really agreed: or they are mutually clear but have formulated their contract, not to suit their own mutual needs, but in uncritical accordance with whatever rules social convention, romantic imagery or undigested idealism suggest to them.

Finally, though this reminder should be unnecessary, we must remember that we have been dealing with personal relationships in their formal aspect only: and none of this must be taken to imply an ideal of such relationships which consists merely of the diligent and pedestrian following of a large number of rules. To borrow a religious example, the mistake of the Pharisees was not that morality is not a rule-governed activity, and does not demand plenty of diligence, hard work and clear formulation. It was rather that the *kind* of rules that should govern relationships between people are not—or not only—those found in the book of Leviticus. Substantial progress in morality and personal relations depends, in fact, upon our being able to formulate as far as possible the skills and intuitive responses on which they depend into a more coherent form, which could hence more easily be learnt and followed.

It is plain enough why the mere formulation of rules is inadequate (or even dangerous), if we consider one or two cases. The obsessional neurotic, for instance, who touches every lamp-post in the road or washes his hands every fifteen minutes, is obeying a very clear and well-formulated set of rules: the objection is that the rules are disconnected with normal human desires and purposes. They achieve no real purpose: their only point is to allay his unconscious fears and guilt-feelings. A great many rules which masquerade as genuinely moral are of this sort. Again, a man might be a great stickler for accuracy, punctuality, tidiness and so forth, and frame rules for these apparently reasonable objectives. But very often he does this because he lacks the security and the spontaneity to live without detailed time-tables and without the certainty of being right in every case: he must know exactly where he is all the time, otherwise he feels lost. Here too the rules are neurotic: that is, designed to meet his own distorted picture of reality rather than reality itself.

We have also the opposite kind of case, in which the rules are sensible but ineffective. A man may know that he ought to be reasonably punctual, and even try hard to be so: but he may nevertheless fail, and always be late for everything. A mother may know that she ought not to lose her temper with her children, or ought not to give preferential treatment to one child rather than another: yet she may be unable to stop doing so. These, like the former, are neurotic cases because they are compulsive. Sometimes the compulsion will be masked by a rationalisation. One might say that hand-washing, or accuracy, or punctuality, is a virtue: and one might say that one ought sometimes to be angry with children, or that one particular child deserves preferential treatment. These rationalisations may, indeed, represent true propositions: nevertheless the actual *motive* for the behaviour is a compulsive and not a rational one. Faced with a situation where it is obvious, even to the individual concerned, that some other kind of behaviour is reasonable, he will still find it difficult or impossible to behave otherwise.

Granted that these are neurotic cases, it would still be useless to prevent the neurotic forcibly from following these rules (except in cases where they harm other people). There is a weak sense in which neurotic symptoms, like physical symptoms, result from the best compromise of which the organism is at the time capable. Given a particular virus in the body, the symptoms of influenza are necessary if the organism is not to collapse completely: and given particular unconscious fears or desires, an obsession or compulsion is (so to speak) the easiest way of the person's mind continuing to survive as a whole. Significant improvement can only be achieved by some process similar to the psychoanalytic, in which we attempt to regain touch with our unconscious minds, and hence to become more aware of our own desires and purposes.

All this is simply to say that until we are clearer about what we really want, our rules (however well formulated) are not likely to prove very satisfactory. But this is an additional reason for clear formulation. We need to be clear about what we think we want, and to have clearly defined rules for getting it, in order to see just how big the gulf is which divides what we think we want from what we really want. It is precisely by the formulation of rules that we come to consider the purposes on which they are supposed to be based; and in this process we can learn to be more honest about these purposes. Formulating rules is only the beginning of the long task of discovering ourselves: but it is a beginning which we can all make, because it can be common ground for all of us—a springboard which our common ability to reason can use to get the whole process off the ground. To ask 'What rules should we have?' immediately involves us in asking 'What is the point of this or that rule?' and if we ask this seriously, and keep on asking it, we are making a significant attempt to be rational, sane, and morally good. Trying to be any one of these three involves us in trying to be the other also: but whichever of them happens to be most appealing to us, it is better to try rather than to resign from the arduous but rewarding business of being a conscious creature.

From Theory to Practice

At a theoretical level, the relationship between conceptual principles and their practical application is comparatively clear. By paying attention to the logic of certain areas of discourse—areas labelled 'punishment', 'equality', 'justice', 'democracy'—we gain a clearer idea of what beliefs and values we can rationally entertain; and here we make use of the philosopher. By paying attention to the empirical facts—crime statistics, voting behaviour, work incentives—we discover by what means we can best put our beliefs and values into practice: and here we make use of the social scientist and other such experts. All this is very well in theory: but in practice it does not happen. Why not? What happens instead? And what can we do about it?

The first thing to notice is that this problem, like so many others, is largely a problem of communication. It is true, of course, that many other factors are involved. Some people are merely stupid, other people are intelligent enough but have vested interests, society as a whole may lack the money to pay for the necessary research, and so forth. But it is also true that we mishandle our existing resources. We have these disciplines—philosophy, sociology, psychology, economics, and others—but we do not organise them properly or make full use of them. They are not efficiently interrelated.

The possibility of research into this problem discloses an apparently vicious circle. Plainly the problem has philosophical, sociological, psychological, economic, and no doubt other aspects: and it could not be solved except by a team of experts in these fields, so as to ensure both that every aspect of the problem was covered, and also that the contributions made by each particular discipline were properly understood by all—for it is just these individual contributions and their interrelations that form the problem. But the mere creation of such a team equipped with this degree of mutual understanding would itself solve the problem, at least in microcosm: for in such a context the proper handling of intellectual resources would *ipso facto* be properly understood. This is hard to achieve, but the degree of understanding and efficiency in communication necessary to create such a team is at least a possibility in some circles: and it is on teams of this kind that I should rest most of my hopes for a solution. Here I can only suggest some of the points which would probably emerge.

First, disagreements are possible at both stages of the process outlined in the first paragraph: that is, we may disagree either about conceptual principles—about the rationality of certain beliefs or values—or about the empirical facts. But since investigating bodies rarely go through each stage consciously, it is nearly always unclear at which stage disagreements arise. For example, even in governmental reports on punishment or sexual morality, it is often hard to tell what the committee thinks (a) about the rationality of a belief in (say) retributive punishment, or state interference with individual morality, and (b) about the sociological and psychological facts. If disagreements arise, one is not sure whether they disagree about the rationality of retribution, or about the crime statistics: about the right of each person to go to hell in his own way, or about the causes of venereal disease and the illegitimate birthrate.

Secondly, it is remarkable that far more experiments in the practical application of concepts are not undertaken, either by official bodies or by private enterprise. Thus, granted that we are very much in the dark about the social and psychological effects of certain types of punishment and reward, education or sexual morality, experiment is one of the most obvious methods of advancing our knowledge. Yet the experimentation in these and other fields is minimal: indeed in some cases, such as sexual behaviour, it is positively forbidden. This is not due entirely to lack of money or other practical difficulties: the causes lie deeper.

Thirdly, since the problems to which these disciplines relate would be agreed by most of us to be at least as important as problems in other fields, it is surprising that these disciplines are not built into our educational system. Educationalists presumably suppose (though I am not sure what the evidence for this supposition is) that the study of Latin grammar, Anglo-Saxon literature, geography, 'religious knowledge', and many other subjects that form part of the curricula of schools and universities is valuable: perhaps because these subjects 'train the mind', perhaps because they are of practical importance in the modern world, or perhaps they enable us to lead more satisfactory lives as human beings with human problems. But on all three of these grounds, particularly the last, there is at least as strong a case for incorporating the disciplines we are discussing. Yet, although at some seats of learning sociology and psychology (as well as philosophy) are fashionable, there has been no serious attempt to put these subjects on the map of secondary and advanced education in general.

This last point gives us some clue to the basic difficulty. It would of course be argued that these disciplines cannot suitably be taught in schools, because of the youth of the pupils and the lack of competent teachers: and these or other arguments could be advanced for the university level. Such arguments are not silly: but those who have experience in this field would agree, I think, that what underlies them is something quite different—a strong feeling that these disciplines are either intellectually disreputable or socially unimportant. It is still widely believed, for instance, that philosophy is a game with words, depth psychology a racket, and sociology a fashionable non-subject. Side by side with this feeling, however, there exists a less commonly expressed but equally powerful attitude: that the disciplines are somehow *dangerous*. Philosophy might lead people astray: depth psychology might drive them mad: sociology might give them funny ideas. This attitude is not so obsolete as might be thought.

This apparent contradiction in attitudes is due to an intense, if largely unconscious, resistance to the disciplines. In order to observe the irrationality of this resistance, we have first to see how far it is reasonable. It is true that the amateur and traditionalist approach displayed in the first attitude, which is particularly strong in England, is a valuable defence against the bogus and the merely fashionable: it is also true that one piece of genuine amateur insight is worth a lot of falsely directed professionalism. Equally, the second attitude properly warns us against philosophy which is little more than an intellectual projection of the philosopher's neuroses, psychoanalysis in which the half-blind are led by the totally sightless, and sociology which is merely an attempt to stir up trouble, appear smart, or give readers the impression of being in the know. Further, the methodology of the social sciences, and indeed of philosophy itself, is much in dispute: and this weakness does indeed greatly diminish the efficiency of these disciplines. To put it roughly, one is never quite sure when one is being told something which is at once novel, true and important, and when one is being kidded. All this and more may be granted.

Nor do I wish to defend those who are expert in these disciplines against such charges as stupidity, dryness, irrelevance, prejudice, neurosis, or any other form of human weakness. For the basic cause of our resistance is doubtless as prevalent in academic circles as elsewhere. This cause is the inability to recognise our own dissatisfactions, or to tolerate them if recognised. One powerful motive for doing moral philosophy, for instance, is the feeling of being lost, uncertain, and in need. Similar motives apply to other disciplines, particularly to depth psychology. We might adduce other motives, such as intellectual curiosity: but if this curiosity were not backed by an admission of some kind of dissatisfaction, it would be a remarkable oddity for a man to spend a great deal of his time on these subjects—just as it is, perhaps, a little odd for a man to devote his life to chess or stamp collecting, interesting though such pursuits might be. Of course the *merits* of such disciplines as philosophy (as opposed to their motivation) depend on their usefulness as techniques. If philosophy is a kind of intellectuals' fantasy, or even a play-therapy which helps nobody except the philosopher himself, then it is largely valueless: and for this reason alone philosophers are well advised to stick closely to the tools of their trade, and not try to sell their neuroses to other people.

But our resistance can be detached, even in cases where we should instinctively deny it. Thus most arguments and discussions arise, as they ought to arise, from practical instances about which we feel strongly. If sufficiently protracted, they lead to a consideration of logical or conceptual points. When these are sorted out, we can re-apply them to the original practical case. But it often happens that somewhere along the line the initial impetus gets lost: the flow of feeling that originally inspired the discussion runs into the sand. It is then that we tend to say that philosophy is boring, or academic, or too difficult, or irrelevant to everyday life. Of course the process needs a lot of hard work to carry through. But if a person can fully recognise and tolerate a need—if he can, as it were, *own up* to its intensity and keep it clearly marked on his emotional register—then the hard work comes of itself. The fact that earning a living is hard work does not deter us, since we have to face our need for food. But where our needs are less visible and less obviously compelling, we often try to pretend that they do not exist, and that we are perfectly all right as we are. The moralist who thinks he already knows what is right and wrong has no time for moral philosophy: the neurotic who persuades himself that he is perfectly happy, or that if he is not it is everyone else's fault, has no time for psychoanalysis.

In the same way, the ability to make serious use of these disciplines depends on the capacity to tolerate doubt: and this in turn depends on the admission of needs. If we need very badly to build a bridge that will enable us to cross a river safely, we shall be more able to tolerate the uncertainties which (until we know how to do it properly) beset bridge-building as an applied science. We shall not be tempted to think we know answers when we do not, or to regard the necessary intellectual work as boring or trivial. A person who makes a premature jump towards a bogus solution, or who gives up hope altogether, has failed to keep his need firmly in his mind. It might be supposed that the intensity of a need or desire might militate against a rational approach—that those who passionately desire health or happiness, for instance, will be likely to invest in some magical solution: perhaps they will take to quack medicines or quack psychology, or invent another world to be happy in if they are miserable in this world. All this is true: but we are talking not merely about the intensity and recognition of needs, but the toleration of them. All false solutions, because they are false, do not satisfy needs: and we only accept them because we pretend that our needs are satisfied when they are not. Lack of the capacity to doubt is a sign of this pretence: we do not allow ourselves to doubt, because we dare not run the risk of being shown up.

If I am on the right lines at all here, it is clearly appropriate to describe this problem, too, as a problem of communication. For the recognition and tolerance of needs, and hence the efficient practice and interrelation of the disciplines we are considering, plainly depend on a context of close personal communication. Without some such appropriate context, the disciplines inevitably become not only dry, but misdirected; and the world becomes divided into a number of intellectuals who are divorced from any real understanding of the primary needs of human beings, and a much larger number of non-intellectuals who are divorced from any real understanding of the necessary intellectual techniques. In its extreme form this divorce leads to the anomalous coexistence, in the same society, of academic political theorists who live in an ivory tower with hysterical mobs and dictators who rampage in the streets.

This sort of situation is possibly more dangerous than we care to suppose. Blessed with a reasonably secure society, and a certain unconscious inheritance of political sanity, most peoples in the western world might regard any improvement as a desirable luxury rather than a matter of urgency. We might think that it would be *nice* if we made better use of our intellectual techniques, because it might solve one or two outstanding social problems of which we are ashamed, and make us feel more educated and progressive. But we may, for all we know, be heading towards a crisis which can only be averted by properly understanding and deploying these techniques. Our psychological capital may be running out, or may be inadequate to cope with a rapidly changing society. Disasters can be invisible as well as material. It may be—though I do not particularly want to prophesy calamity—that such phenomena as increased crime and juvenile delinquency, anxiety and neurosis, are symptoms that herald unimagined changes in our society: changes that we shall regret, as we have regretted so many changes, only when it is too late.

In this context also the notion of equality has a large part to play. For all instances of bad communication, inability to engage in effective rational discussion, and incapacity to tolerate needs, also appear as instances of a failure to maintain equality-relationships. The context of rational discussion, like many other contexts, demands the ability to relate to another person as to an equal: to play a particular game or rule-governed activity without finding it intolerable. Only too often we move away from such contexts before giving them a chance to satisfy our needs, by regressing into anger, boredom or complete detachment. It is to be expected that men like Socrates and Jesus will attract our most bitter hostility, because we are not emotionally capable of playing the games which they want us to play. Because we are incapable of a relationship of equality with them, even in the context of teaching and learning, we feel ourselves inferior (though we may represent this feeling to ourselves as a conscious superiority): we react by saying that they are 'complacent', 'inhuman', 'too idealistic', 'impractical', 'too logical', 'boring', 'commonplace' or 'unsympathetic'.

It is important to appreciate that those who crucify or administer hemlock are not significantly different from ourselves. When we are asked to play their games, but find ourselves incapable, we react as a child reacts when it is told to do something by its father but cannot do it properly. Heroes and charismatic figures, like Hitler or the late President Kennedy, or even a symbolic figure of a weaker kind, such as a consitutional monarch, require no such effort from us. We need only warm to them, partially identify ourselves and our interests with them, follow them, show them loyalty, and so forth. We regress quite happily to a primitive form of love. By contrast the Socrates-Jesus type does not act as a mere image, but makes demands on us. If we cannot fulfil them, we regress to a primitive form of hate, whose violence it is hard to overestimate. Much as the patient under psychoanalysis will on many occasions regard his analyst as a diabolical persecutor, as inhuman, unsympathetic and complacent, or as a proper target for the most passionate hatred and contempt, so we project our own feelings of hostility and inadequacy upon other people, when we are unable to relate effectively to them or to meet the demands of a particular context. Like the analyst, they are dummy figures which we stuff with our own feelings.

Of course this does not only apply to the context of rational discussion: as we saw in the last section, there are plenty of other games which are equally important, and which our own inability to play may provoke feelings of equal violence in us. The kind of rational discussion which relates to the disciplines we are considering, however, may be thought to have a particular importance of its own, in that it is the most delicate and sophisticated, and hence potentially the most efficient, tool of communication that we possess. It acquires this delicacy, not by excluding personal emotion altogether, but by using it *as its subject-matter*. Because of the violence of their emotions, and their lack of training, most people are unable to regard their own emotions (or any problem connected at all closely with them) as mere subject-matter for any great length of time: rational discussion, in this sense, breaks down, and they fly to *ad hominem* arguments insults, anger, boredom, tears, and so on. Directly opposed to this fault, which might be described as the vulgar error, is the academic error of divorcing rational discussion from personal emotion altogether—of not allowing it to enter the arena even as subject-matter to be examined. Any effective rational consideration must involve the three-fold process of being able to feel emotion, being able to tolerate it, and being able to organise it by the use of the intelligence. Without a proper understanding of this process the amount of wastage in any form of significant learning is bound to be very considerable.

If ever we tackle this problem effectively at all, it will be largely because a number of individuals become more able to tolerate their own needs, and hence to set up contexts of communication for themselves and for others which will accelerate a solution. Such individuals will pay more than usual attention to the disciplines which we have discussed; but we must not wait for those who are expert in these disciplines to tell us what to do. One reason for this is that different individuals and different contexts vary so greatly that the person concerned is often the best possible expert for his own case. But a more important reason is that the rules of communication depend for their point on our own wills and desires, and have to be formulated in terms of our own wills and desires: and consequently only we ourselves can, logically, judge the efficacy of the rules. They are our rules, and we must invent, operate, overhaul and assess them. A choice of rules and contexts of communication is, in effect, a choice of a way of living: nobody can make this sort of choice for us. Philosophers may make the sort of general points I have been making, and psychologists may add important facts which will give the points more substance: but if we allow philosophers or psychologists to do our work for us, we shall merely have adopted one more defence, another form of resistance to committing ourselves to the task of communicating. To abandon this task is to abandon not only a belief in human equality, but a belief in humanity itself.